Classic Hammond Organ

KNOW THE PLAYERS, PLAY THE MUSIC

Steve Lodder

Classic Hammond Organ

Steve Lodder

A BACKBEAT BOOK
First edition 2008
Published by Backbeat Books
(an imprint of Hal Leonard Corporation)
19 West 21st Street,
New York, NY 10010, USA
www.backbeatbooks.com

Devised and produced for Backbeat Books by Outline Press Ltd
2A Union Court, 20-22 Union Road, London SW4 6JP, England
www.backbeatuk.com

ISBN: 978-0-87930-929-9

EDITOR: John Morrish
DESIGN: Paul Cooper Design

Origination and print by Colorprint (Hong Kong)

08 09 10 11 12 5 4 3 2 1

Contents

Wild Bill Davis (above) discovered the Hammond organ in 1950, forming his first organ trio a year later. Fats Waller (top right), best known as a pianist, recorded on Hammond in the early 1940s. Count Basie (bottom right) was another occasional organist.

Classic Hammond

THE
INSTRUMENT

THE HAMMOND TONEWHEEL ORGAN is like no other instrument. It's a living, wheezing, whirring thing that can scream, wail, and growl. It can be reverent, irreverent, cheesy, sophisticated, funky, and more. It is full of character, each individual instrument having its own foibles and peccadilloes, weaknesses and strengths, each capable of glorious, spine-tingling music.

Turning on

Now imagine you are walking into a top-notch studio, with the producer murmuring something about "trying out a spot of Hammond on that track". You glance over and spy a beautiful, if slightly intimidating, B-3 or similar and realise that while you might have used Hammond sounds in synths and samplers over the years you have never been confronted by the real thing. A sense of nervousness creeps in, a slight breaking of sweat, first at the back of the neck, then a flush spreading to the chest. Not wishing to be seen as lacking in expertise, you wander over and profess intimate knowledge of the start-up process, drawbar operation, and presets, when the truth is quite different.

Should you be a complete novice, this is all you need to know to proceed with confidence. Firstly, there is the start-up process. You should find two switches, the left marked Start and the right Run. To get the tonewheels up to optimum speed, hold the Start switch up for the time it takes to spell out H—A—M—M—O—N—D (at a leisurely 60 bpm), then engage the Run switch, so that you're holding both. Spell O—R—G—A—N and let go of the Start switch, then the Run switch. You are in business.

The next potential pitfall is understanding the special keys to the left of each manual, which have the normal black and white reversed, like on a harpsichord: the white keys are black and the sharps and flats are white. These are not keys you play but switches that activate preset settings of the drawbars that control the instrument's timbre. There are two sets of nine drawbars for each manual. To use the drawbars themselves, rather than the preset sounds, you press either of the two right-most 'harpsichord' keys, B and B-flat, which activate the left or right set of drawbars for that manual. To convince a neutral observer of your suitability to operate the machinery, select the B preset on the upper manual and pull towards you the three drawbars to the left, all the way out. There are some rocker switches to the right of you that control percussion. Select on/normal/fast/third. By this point you should be ready to engage your fingers with the keys of the upper manual and run off a few blues lines: it's that classic jazz vibe.

Next up is to display your familiarity with the Leslie speaker switch, down on the edge of the case just to the left. This should be set to Slow, but holding a chord and throwing back your head while grimacing with emotion and switching up to Fast will really turn people's heads. Try not to hold this pose for too long; return the switch to Slow and revert to your normal, cooler demeanour.

And that should be mission accomplished. You can spend the next half hour figuring out the rest in a supercharged voyage of discovery. That's not to say that the journey ends there; in comparative terms you've just gone 100 yards down the road when there's the whole world to explore. There are still plenty of unexplained parameters that need clarification, but only after a look at the Hammond from a historical perspective.

Laurens Hammond and the tonewheel principle

Electric instruments weren't wholly new when Laurens Hammond began toying with the idea of an electric organ that could replace pipe organs in churches for a fraction of the price. The first electronic instrument, meaning one in which the sound is created by an oscillator, was the Theremin, invented in Russia in 1919, which is controlled by hand movements in the air rather than a keyboard. It found its way firstly into orchestral music, then film music, and eventually into rock and pop. Dmitri Shostakovich wrote for the instrument, and Jimmy Page played one on 'Whole Lotta Love'. (I don't think the two ever performed together.)

Dr Friedrich Trautwein's Trautonium, invented around 1929, was also wholly electronic, but controlled by a wire stretched over a metal rail. This caught the attention of composer Paul Hindemith, among others. But the instrument that most closely prefigures the technology used in the Hammond was the Telharmonium, an extraordinary behemoth that weighed about 200 tons in its second incarnation, was 60 feet long, and occupied a whole floor of 'Telharmonic Hall' in New York City.

The man responsible for this monster was one Thadeus Cahill, who built it between 1897 and 1906. Although there were problems with the design, the instrument included elements that were later to become commonplace. The most important of these was additive synthesis, a term that applies equally to the

Hammond organ. The basic principle of operation was the use of a series of motors to rotate discs with notches or teeth around the edge. These 'tonewheels' lined up with electro-magnetic pickups that were sensitive to the magnetic field of the wheel. When the wheel turned, the fluctuations in the field were picked up by the coil pickup, inducing a varying voltage. The number of notches and speed of tonewheel rotation determined the frequency of the variation and hence the pitch of the note.

The instrument was polyphonic, with keyboards to control the pitch and duration, and its frequency range was from 40Hz to 4kHz. The problem was how to hear it; this was several decades before amplification technology. Early attempts at using piano soundboards to amplify the sound were abandoned in favour of connecting the machine to the local telephone network and using large paper cones attached to ordinary telephone receivers as primitive loudspeakers. However, other users of that phone network were liable to be interrupted by loud yet ethereal electronic sounds that drowned out normal conversation. The plan had been to pipe the music to hotels, theatres, and even private homes, but by 1914 Cahill's business had gone bankrupt.

But despite the problems of audibility, the idea of producing sound from tonewheels was a good one. The tonewheels produced sine waves, which are pure fundamental tones with little or nothing in the way of upper harmonic frequencies. This is a limitation, as most instruments produce their distinctive sound through the presence of a particular mixture of higher harmonics or 'upper partials'. Cahill's solution was 'additive synthesis', which meant adding more tonewheels at higher pitches, effectively adding harmonics to the original sine wave, and therefore changing the character of the resulting sound.

It is hard to tell what the Telharmonium sounded like, as no recordings exist, but reportedly it did a good job of simulating acoustic instruments such as the cello, clarinet, and flute. As far as repertoire goes, the instrument was mainly used for playing classical music by the likes of Bach, Chopin, and Grieg. But the composer Ferruccio Busoni glimpsed the future in the technology, referring to it in his *Sketch Of A New Aesthetic Of Music*, published in 1911. He includes an interesting word of caution: "Only a long and careful series of experiments, and a continued training of the ear, can render this unfamiliar material approachable and plastic for the coming generation, and for Art." The possibilities he saw for electronic instruments in modern music were not to be realised for another 50 years or so.

If Busoni was the musical visionary, Laurens Hammond was the pragmatic

Wired for sound: the Hammond A-100, with its built-in loudspeakers, being played live by the great Jimmy Smith.

inventor. A brilliant engineer from an early age, he managed to come up with a design for automatic transmission in cars (Renault rejected it) and a patent for a new improved barometer even before getting his degree in mechanical engineering at Cornell University. He began his career with the McCord Radiator Company in Detroit, Michigan, then served with the American Expeditionary Force in France during World War One. He subsequently joined the Gray Motor Company, a manufacturer of marine and automobile engines.

Hammond had always wanted to be an independent inventor and in 1920 he began developing his own ideas. The first was a 'tickless' clock, created by putting the mechanism in a soundproof box. Then he began working on a system for making and showing 3D films. The system, called Teleview, was installed in the Selwyn Theatre in New York City and a special feature film (*M.A.R.S* or *The Man From M.A.R.S*) made for it. It was a complicated system using two cameras, one for each eye, two projectors, and a motorised viewer attached to each seat that directed the image to each eye in turn.

The system depended upon Hammond's most important invention, a synchronous motor that revolved in phase with the newly standardised 60Hz alternating current domestic power supply and kept everything in sync. Technically impressive, the system was a commercial flop. People liked the novelty but not the film, and the show closed in less than a month. Then Hammond developed a system of projecting 3D shadow images of live performers for the Ziegfeld Follies stage show of 1923. This used the now-familiar red and green glasses and was so successful that it was pirated all over the world.

His big breakthrough, however, came with the launch in 1928 of the Hammond Clock Company. The clock in question was driven by the synchronous motor, and soon profits were soaring, but not for long. Other companies jumped on the bandwagon and competition was rife. Another invention, an electric bridge table that shuffled and dealt the cards, did well, selling 14,000 units in 1932 alone. But the Depression came along and soon Hammond was desperate to find new uses for his synchronous motor.

Strange noises were soon emanating from a phonograph and other devices on the third and fourth floors of the clock company. Ear-shattering squeakings and low frequencies chimed in, causing the building to tremble. Hammond had turned his hand, and his remarkable brain, to the production of musical sounds. One day Hammond asked one of his employees, a church organist on Sundays, whether he'd heard anything unusual that day. The man answered that he'd heard a sound resembling a flute. Hammond replied, "Well, I've just made an electric flute."

The synchronous motor powered a tonewheel, with its cogs and bumps revolving past an pickup assembly, made from a magnet and a coil, that picked up the fluctuating current and took it to a radio amplifier. That raised the level of the signal before kicking it out to a loudspeaker, which then moved the air on its way to the listener's ears and the end of the journey – the perception of sound. It was a long and winding road from those early experiments to the refinement of the first prototype in 1933, but the organ, or 'packing box prototype' as it was known, made quite a splash. The patent was granted on the April 24th 1934. Around this time a pair of engineers sent by Henry Ford himself had come to check out the idea. When Ford himself was given a demonstration of the first instrument, he ordered six.

Interest from all sorts of corners followed, and not exclusively from the church and classical music fraternities. George Gershwin put in an order pretty quickly at the 1935 Industrial Arts Exposition, and Albert Schweitzer, Sigmund Romberg (composer of *The Desert Song*), and the conductor Fritz Reiner were among those queuing up to play the Hammond organ. In the first year, 1,400 orders were placed for organs priced at $1,250 each. Churches jumped at the chance to install an instrument at a fraction of the cost of a pipe organ, even though the sound was far from identical. Hammond was keen to push the

> STRANGE NOISES WERE SOON EMANATING FROM THE THIRD AND FOURTH FLOORS OF THE CLOCK COMPANY. HAMMOND HAD TURNED TO MAKING MUSICAL SOUNDS.

instrument's ability to recreate pipe organ sounds. According to the first advertisement, the organ "is built to conform to established pipe organ standards, requires pipe organ technique of the musician who plays it, and produces the entire range of tone colouring necessary for the rendition, without sacrifice, of the great works of organ literature". The ad also boasts of other sounds never before heard.

As the Telharmonium is to the Hammond organ, so the hydraulis is to the pipe organ. Invented in Alexandria, Egypt, close to 250BC, the Greek organ used water pressure to regulate the hand-pumped air supply. Keys – the hydraulis was the first known keyboard instrument – sent the air to what must have looked like a row of panpipes, which subsequently developed into brass pipes which may have had reeds. From Greece the instrument spread to Rome, where the hydraulis was used at ceremonies and gladiatorial spectacles: the Emperor Nero apparently fancied himself as a performer.

Despite being an amazing technological feat, the water system was soon ditched in favour of a simpler mechanism based on air bellows and a flexible air reservoir, which are the basis of the pipe organ. In early medieval times, the size and sophistication of organs increased rapidly. The 10th century organ at Winchester Cathedral in England was said to have 400 pipes, requiring 70 fit men to operate its 26 bellows and two organists to play the two keyboards. It would have been audible from a long distance. By the 15th century, organs incorporated pedals plus a variety of sounds, or stops. The next 200 years saw the expansion of the sound palette as the instrument reached what many would consider to be its ideal design in the Baroque period.

To return to additive synthesis, the pipe organ is analogous to the synthesizer, in that sounds of different frequencies, usually related in the harmonic series, are combined to produce elaborate tone colours. The system used is worth investigation as it leads eventually to the Hammond. The basic building block is the 8′ (eight-foot) pipe, which plays C3 (middle C) when you play C3. So far so logical. The 16′ sounds an octave lower, the 4′ an octave higher, and so on. To describe this in terms of the harmonic series, the C3 is the fundamental, the 16′ is the sub-fundamental and the 4′ is the second harmonic. Higher harmonics are used also, displaying strange and exotic numbers such as 1 3/5′ or 2 2/3′. Opposite you can see a full table of pipes for C3.

The single main difference between a pipe organ and a Hammond tonewheel organ is this: on the pipe organ, combinations of stops/harmonics are always coloured by the type of pipe (which could be a reed, flute, etc), while combinations on the Hammond are pretty much assembled from pure sine waves by additive synthesis. This makes it easier for the ear to perceive upper harmonic additions as a change of tone colour rather than as a completely separate sound.

So what controls the tone change? A system of nine drawbars, controlling the stops as shown in the table opposite. Each drawbar has a volume setting, from 'off' (fully in) through to eight (fully out), so if you wanted to play just the fundamental, you would pull drawbar three out to maximum and away you go. This system virtually defines the tonewheel organ, and underpins all Hammond models from the organ's inception to later keyboard/module emulations.

Drawbar settings are normally annotated using numbers in a row. 888888888, for instance, would mean that every stop was on maximum. Note that the white drawbars are the octaves. Adding other intervals will effectively add a transposed line of notes; a pretty odd effect if heard without proper balancing against the fundamentals.

Pipe organ stop	MIDI note	Harmonic series	Drawbar
16' pipe	C2	sub fundamental	1
5 1/3' pipe	G2	sub 3rd harmonic	2
8' pipe	C3	fundamental	3
4' pipe	C4	2nd harmonic	4
2 2/3' pipe	G4	3rd harmonic	5
2' pipe	C5	4th harmonic	6
1 3/5' pipe	E5	5th harmonic	7
1 1/3' pipe	G5	6th harmonic	8
1' pipe	C6	8th harmonic	9

The Model A, launched in April 1935, cemented the layout of Hammonds to come, incorporating two 61-key manuals and a pedal board of 25 notes (that's just two octaves, to keep the costs down), arranged similarly to those on a church organ. A swell or expression pedal controlled the volume of the organ, providing a hefty 40dB of attenuation. To the left of each of the two manuals were 12 hard-wired preset keys, set out like a harpsichord keyboard, the lowest (C) cancelling all the drawbars, and the top two (B-flat and B) switching on the two sets of drawbars for each manual. Thus to enable the drawbars associated with the upper manual, you would press B-flat for the set on the left, and B for the set on the right. The same with the lower manual. Other presets provided church organ registrations of varying effectiveness. The pedal section had just two drawbars, an 8' and a 16'. Variations of chorus and tremolo effect were also built in, to enable the organ to sound more like a church organ.

Meanwhile, the market was on the move. Ice rinks and race tracks were soon targeted for sales. Radio stations acquired their own resident organists. Milt Herth, of Indiana station WIND, was one of the first Hammond characters, recording 'Stomping At The Savoy' in 1936. The story of the Hammond includes many women practitioners, and right there at the start was Ethel Smith. She paid her dues first on Caribbean and South American cruises and later at the Copacabana club in Rio de Janeiro, where she combined organ and Brazilian flavours into a veritable sundae of sound. She discovered the Hammond as early as 1935, and took to it like a duck to a pond. Her recording of 'Tico Tico' sold over two million copies, but more importantly, illustrated a real understanding of the instrument's capabilities. Techniques such as switching rapidly from manual to manual, or holding notes and toggling presets, were swiftly incorporated into Hammond style.

A movie clip of 'Tico Tico' (from the 1944 Hollywood film *Bathing Beauty*) is still around, and shows off a suitably attractive collection of female performers re-creating the 'exotic' ambience of Brazilian 'choro' style. Smith certainly had a very crisp technique, an incredibly neat 'staccato' or detached note style, no doubt assisted by the fact that the Hammond is not a weighted keyboard like the piano, having an action more like that a modern synthesizer. She placed a huge importance on articulation in her instructional books, something that classical organ players know all about. When an instrument does not permit you to vary volume by touch you have to shape lines and phrases through note duration. In other words, you

> YOU CAN'T BASH THE KEYS HARDER FOR EXPRESSION, SO YOU HAVE TO SCULPT THE LENGTH OF THE NOTES INSTEAD. SHORT NOTES ARE LESS IMPORTANT THAN LONG ONES.

can't bash it harder for expression so you have to sculpt the length of the notes instead. The general rule is that a shorter note has less musical importance than a longer one – scream for longer and you're more likely to be heard. Ethel Smith went on to work with the likes of Bing Crosby and Frank Sinatra, becoming the first true star of the Hammond.

Jazz keyboardists were also sitting up and taking note. Fats Waller considered the piano to be his main instrument, but at the age of 15 one of his first sources of musical income was playing the organ in a Harlem cinema. By the late 1920s he was recording on a pipe organ, which for all its purity swings like the devil incarnate. 'St. Louis Blues' never sounded like this before, and the gorgeous 'Lenox Avenue Blues', also known as 'Church Organ Blues' has pre-echoes of Joe Zawinul's synth work with Weather Report. No wonder, then, that Fats was an early attender at the Hammond party; the early 1940s saw him recording tunes such as 'Clarinet Marmalade' with a jazz horn line-up and plenty of organ glissandi in addition to the ever-present urgent swing. There is even a version of his great hit, 'Jitterbug Waltz', played on Hammond.

Fats Waller had a pupil, one William 'Count' Basie, who, having started with a pair of sticks in his hands, dropped them and turned first to piano and then to organ: "I had dropped into the old Lincoln Theater in Harlem, and I heard a young fellow beating it out on an organ. From that time on, I was a daily customer, hanging on to every note, sitting behind him all the time. He got used to seeing me, as though I were part of the show. One day he asked me whether I played the organ. 'No,' I said, 'but I'd give my right arm to learn.'"[1]

Bill Basie was soon sitting alongside the master, soaking up the style and content. Known for his spare piano style, he became an occasional organist. There are a few recordings from 1952. He recorded as a sideman with Basie bandmember Paul Quinichette in January, and tracks were released on Quinichette's albums *The Vice 'Pres'* and *The Complete Paul Quinichette*. And he made an album with his own big band, *Count At The Organ*. The track 'K. C. Organ Blues' (which is also on *Verve Jazz Masters Vol. 2*) displays a skill with the volume pedal that sounds as if it could well have been acquired in the cinema. Alternating between small trills and juicy two-hander chords, the track swirls languidly through a 12-bar sequence.

Less of a Hammond part-timer was Wild Bill Davis, an organist who was later to work with the other great jazz bandleader of the era, Duke Ellington. Davis did a stretch in the late 1940s with Louis Jordan and discovered the Hammond in 1950, forming an organ trio the next year. At least, that's one version: Jimmy Smith claimed to have heard him on organ in the 1930s. Either way, Davis was the undisputed pioneer of the organ trio. His first line-up consisted of Floyd Smith on guitar and Chris Columbus on drums, and his sound is best sampled on the set of five albums made with Everest records from 1959-61.

What Davis does is to play like a big band (it sounds like it's modelled on Basie), using the two-hander block chord technique that George Shearing applied to the piano; and very effective it is too. The power and energy of big band phrasing is present, even if diluted by emanating from one sound source. Less effective to these 21st-century ears are the jazz tracks. Thelonius Monk's 'Round Midnight', available on *The Everest Years*, is crushed somewhat beneath a combination of the weight of sound and the straightness of the 16th-note phrasing. Still, he's capable of devastating runs; when the guitarist takes up the main tune, Davis's right hand rips right to left across the upper manual.

After teaming up with master Ellington saxophonist Johnny Hodges, Davis toured and recorded with the Duke Ellington band, but again I feel subtlety is rather cast to the wind in this context. Video of a concert performance of 'Satin Doll' in Berlin in 1969 – on YouTube at the time of writing – bears this out. After the band have played the head (the main theme of the piece), Davis is given his solo spot, which consists of playing two-hand passages in rather stock voicings, which seems a letdown after the originality of the opening.

It would come as no surprise to find out that the gospel churches were early customers for the Hammond; the combination of price and novelty must have been an irresistible mix. The great gospel singer Mahalia Jackson flourished through the 1940s, and by the time of her big recording contracts, in the 1950s, her line-up inevitably included an organ alongside the equally necessary piano, guitar, bass, and drums. Gospel music is still one of the thriving arenas for B-3 action. More on that later.

Take yourself back into a world without synthesizers, samplers, computers, or any of that stuff, and imagine what an impact the Hammond must have created. How many times have you seen the phrase "limitless possibilities" used in advertisements for synths and instruments and boxes in general? Well, Hammond had to back off from claiming the organ could produce "an infinite number of tones", after a legal action brought by pipe organ manufacturers – they hoped to prevent Hammond calling its instrument an organ at all – but the scope for sonic exploration must have felt vast. Hammond was also improving the product; churches were lacking fullness and depth in the sound, so a chorus generator using a second tonewheel was added, with various settings.

Want your Hammond to sound like a marimba? No problem. In 1955, Hammond introduced a 'Percussion' control. It doesn't entirely convince as a marimba, but nevertheless gives a hefty clunk to the front end of the note. And guess what, not only does it add edge to solo lines, it sounds funky. Available only on the upper manual preset B, you can choose whether the clunk emphasises the second or the third harmonic (which has repercussions for the brightness of the effect), you can have a fast or a normal decay, and you can have it soft or normal.

Mr Hammond can't have known quite the stir the percussion module would cause; lives would be changed. The instruments that many would consider to be the classic Hammonds (with percussion), filtered on to the market from January 1955 onwards and were in production until December 1974. The B-3, C-3 and A-100 were identical in sound generation. The case of the C-3 was wrapped around all the way to the floor for church use, while the A-100 had its speaker system built into the case rather than contained in a separate enclosure. Which leads us into the whole question of speakers, and the last piece of the jigsaw when it comes to readying the instrument for the coming Hammond jazz explosion.

> IN 1955, HAMMOND INTRODUCED A 'PERCUSSION' CONTROL. IT DOESN'T ENTIRELY CONVINCE AS A MARIMBA, BUT NEVERTHELESS GIVES A HEFTY CLUNK TO THE FRONT END OF A NOTE.

Don Leslie and the Leslie speaker

The Leslie speaker cabinet has become inseparable from the Hammond organ, to the extent that you wouldn't seriously consider owning the one without the other. Once you've swum in a swirling ocean of Doppler-effect sound, you'll never forget it. What's even more amazing is that it's something you can *play*; switching in the effect can be as dramatic and musical as playing another bunch of notes.

Hammond speaker cabinets were originally nothing fancy. If anything, they emphasised the flatness of the early organ's sound compared to that of a pipe organ, which diffuses in all directions, depending on the positioning of the various ranks of pipes. In 1937, Don Leslie was a radio engineer, living in Los Angeles. The frequency of the electricity supply in parts of California had changed from 50Hz to 60Hz, and Leslie was employed to go to the homes of Hammond customers and modify their organs to suit the new system. He bought an organ of his own, but decided he could do better than the standard speaker. Over the next three years he built several prototypes of a speaker cabinet incorporating a rotating horn and drum, arriving at a finished design in 1940. He called it the Vibratone.

The Leslie cabinet depends on the Doppler effect, in which the pitch of a sound changes as it moves relative to the listener. We hear that effect every time a car passes us: the pitch of the engine sound rises as the car approaches and then falls as it passes. That's what the rotating horn is doing. It introduces frequency modulation, raising the frequency of the sound as the horn comes towards the listener and lowering it as it moves away. But there's also amplitude modulation going on, because the volume fluctuates depending on whether the horn is pointing at you or away from you. The result is the Leslie cabinet's inimitable wash of sound.

There are two popular models of Leslie cabinet, the 122 and the 147. Of these the 122 is the most frequently used, having been specifically designed for Hammond organs, though at 41 inches tall it's no shrinking violet. The 147 is identical in cabinet and speaker specification, but the amplifier input is adapted to enable it to work with a variety of makes of organ, or even electric pianos. In each case, the wooden cabinet comprises three compartments. The lower section houses the 40-watt power amp and the lower frequency wooden rotor. That's going to move the low end. The middle section contains the crossover network, which separates high and low frequencies, the 15-inch bass speaker that's directed down to the lower rotor, and the high frequency speaker. The sound from the high frequency driver passes through to a horn that revolves at high speed. A second dummy horn, not connected to the driver, points in the opposite direction to balance the mechanism. Louvres at top and bottom release the sound. Note that the speakers themselves do not revolve: both high and low frequency loudspeakers pass sound to revolving elements that swirl it around.

If you've spotted the amplifier power rating of the 122 and 147, you will wonder how the Leslie cabinet can compete with electric guitars in a rock context. With difficulty, is the short answer. Many Leslies have been beefed up in the amp and speaker departments in search of a level playing field. It is easy enough to take the sides off the cabinet in order to provide sonic clarity and an increase in volume; some people even claim that revealing the rotor provides visual interest.

The switches to control the Leslie are normally down to the left of the lower manual of the organ, but it can also be operated by a footswitch. These can be problematic, though: I recently had to go through an audio file removing loud clicks whenever the footswitch was pressed. There are two speeds, 'Slow' or 'Chorale', and 'Fast' or 'Tremolo'. It may also be possible to stop the motors completely, depending on the model. Stopping the rotor can be useful to give the bass end more focus.

There are many ways to record the Hammond/Leslie setup. One simple but effective method is to use a single microphone up close (but far enough away to escape the wind rush of the rotors) with the volume cranked up. Keeping the louvres in position helps to minimize the wind noise. If you're going stereo, then use two microphones at the top, panned left and right with another taking care of bass. But why skimp on stereo on the bass end? It is moving, after all.

In the end it's all about taste. Rudy Van Gelder combined good taste with engineering expertise. As engineer for Blue Note, he was responsible for the way we hear a huge amount of jazz from that era. In 1959 he established his studio at Englewood Cliffs, New Jersey, and he still operates it today, re-mastering Blue Note's catalogue into 24-bit digital versions. The studio did not record exclusively for Blue Note. Impulse made John Coltrane's masterpiece, *A Love Supreme*, there. Verve recorded Jimmy Smith there, Prestige recorded Jack McDuff, and just about everyone on the jazz scene used the studio at some time or another.

Van Gelder is secretive about his techniques, but his setup for Leslie involved using a stereo pair of microphones for the treble. For the bass, he would take the signal from the Hammond into the desk via direct injection, take the top off it so just the bass was left and mix it back with the sound from the stereo pair. The result was a tight bass end. Of course, you can put other devices through Leslie speakers: guitars (The Beatles' 'While My Guitar Gently Weeps', Hendrix's 'Little

Wing'); pianos (Pink Floyd's 'Echoes' and 'Atom Heart Mother'); and even vocals (again The Beatles, with 'Tomorrow never knows', and The Grateful Dead's 'Rosemary').

So why did Hammond and Leslie never join forces on the commercial level? One answer could be that Hammond was never an enthusiast for the washy Leslie sound, preferring the cleaner option provided by his own speakers. Another possibility is that Hammond was unable to distinguish between the two systems. With no musical ability, he never showed much interest in the musical side of the organ's development, leaving it to others with better ears.

Don Leslie's concept was to make the organ sound more like a theatre organ, of which the mighty Wurlitzer was the prime example. The organ Fats Waller played in the theatre would probably have been a Wurlitzer. More than 2,000 were built to satisfy demand during the silent movie era. In the 1930s, if it wasn't an orchestra or a piano accompanying the film, it would be a Wurlitzer, an instrument designed to display all the timbral versatility of an orchestra for a fraction of the cost. If you've heard a Wurlitzer, you'll know that it has a similar level of swooshiness to the Leslie sound. But it seems Laurens Hammond wasn't a fan.

A CERTAIN AMOUNT OF PROFESSIONAL PRIDE WAS AT STAKE. IN 1940, LESLIE DEMONSTRATED THE SPEAKER TO HAMMOND BUT IT DID NOT RESPOND.

There was also a certain amount of professional pride at stake. In 1940, Leslie demonstrated the speaker to Hammond and gave the company 30 days to license it. Hammond did not respond, so Leslie established his own company, Electro Music. The 'Vibratone' became the 'Leslie Vibratone' and finally the 'Leslie' in 1949. Leslie boasted that demand was so great that he had never had to advertise his product.

The rivalry between Hammond and Leslie remained intense while the two men were running things, but since then the two companies have come together. Leslie sold his Electro Music to CBS in 1965, which sold it to Hammond in 1980. Hammond was bankrupted in 1985, and its name and designs were bought by Noel Crabbe, an Australian investor. He in turn sold Hammond to Suzuki and Leslie to the Calo Corporation in Illinois. Finally, in 1991, Leslie was repurchased by Hammond/Suzuki USA. Today the company makes a range of Leslie speakers, including the famous 122 and 147.

Keith Emerson (above) proved himself a brilliant Hammond player –
as well as a consummate showman – with The Nice and Emerson,
Lake & Palmer. Tori Amos (top right) took up the organ after
receiving a B-3 as a Christmas gift from her husband. Sly Stone
(bottom right) is a multi-instrumentalist who used Hammond to
good effect in the 1960s with his band The Family Stone.

Classic Hammond

THE
PLAYERS

SOMETIMES the right circumstances just have to be in place for someone extraordinary to take advantage of them. An instrument, a style of music, a recording medium, all await the arrival of someone with the foresight to pounce on the opportunity. In the case of the Hammond organ, that man was Jimmy Smith. He was to record more than 80 albums under his own name in a career spanning more than 50 years, and to a majority of music listeners he personifies the Hammond organ. There would be others: Brother Jack McDuff, Richard 'Groove' Holmes, Charles Earland, Don Patterson. Each had his own angle, but none matched the musical purpose displayed on the Blue Note and Verve recordings of Jimmy Smith.

The first jazz wave

Jazz or jazz-influenced music was in the midst of renewal and development in the 1950s. Bebop, the intricate, furious language of Charlie Parker and the early Miles Davis, was giving way to the next wave of jazz, 'hard bop'. It used the same adventurous soloing devices as bebop, but widened the groove possibilities to include straighter rhythm & blues feels. Often the tunes themselves were more riff-based, providing an easier bed for the listener to stretch out on.

The jazz pianist Horace Silver was in Miles Davis's quintet in 1954 when it recorded (in Rudy Van Gelder's studio) the tunes 'Airegin', 'Oleo', Doxy', and 'But Not For Me'. In his autobiography, *Miles*, Davis recalled that he was looking for a "a more funky kind of blues"[2]. That's why Silver was there; he had just cut his teeth with a trio recording of his own compositions using gospel and funk-tinged grooves, and Miles, in his inimitable way, could spot a new direction a mile off at least. The bluesy 'Opus De Funk' provides the clue for that direction. It's not funk in the 1960s sense, but what Dizzy Gillespie describes as a sound that reasserted "the primacy of rhythm & blues in our music and made you get funky to play it…. Hard bop, with its more earthy, churchy sound, drew a lot of new black fans to our music."[3] Call it funky, call it rootsy, call it soulful, call it a precursor to rock'n'roll maybe, but a more accessible jazz style was arriving, and it would be recorded largely by Blue Note.

The incomparable Jimmy Smith at the B-3.

1956 was quite a year for Jimmy Smith. He released five albums, starting with volumes one and two of *A New Sound, A New Star: Jimmy Smith At The Organ*. They were followed by *The Incredible Jimmy Smith At The Organ*, and it was still only June. Then came two live albums, volumes one and two of *The Incredible Jimmy Smith At Club Baby Grand*, and it was not yet August. Not much time for margaritas by the pool that summer, but you have to take advantage of the market while people are interested in you, and interested they were.

It all started with this: "Part of it was that I was just sick of out-of-tune pianos! You never knew what you were gonna get in those clubs. I knew a lot of cats who carried a tuning fork with 'em and tuned the piano on opening night if they had to. The organ, it never goes out of tune."[4] Both his parents were pianists, so Smith probably knew a thing or two about piano tuning.

Born in 1925 in Norristown, Pennsylvania, Smith received a grounding at his father's knee, then studied in nearby Philadelphia at the Hamilton School of Music (1948), where his instrument was double bass, and the Ornstein School of Music (1949-50). The city had a lively jazz and jazz organ scene. Players of the calibre of Bill Doggett (who had discovered the Hammond in the very early 1950s) and Milt Buckner (later Lionel Hampton's organist) were gigging around. Smith was an accomplished jazz pianist, but in 1953 he got the chance to hear and meet Wild Bill Davis and decided to take up the Hammond. Davis kindly told the aspiring organist that it would take him ten years just to learn the pedals. But Smith wasn't put off; the remark only served to increase his resolve to master the instrument.

Smith says he learned a lot from pianists, the left hands of Bud Powell and Art Tatum in particular: "Tatum, Fats Waller, all the stride guys, they mixed crazy left-hand bass with their playing, and if you really wanna understand the jazz B-3 thing, you should check them out."[5] He said this about going to see Tatum: "His left hand was so fast it was like a gliss, and he kept it all goin' – bass and chords – while he drank a beer with his right. Best time I ever had in my life. Didn't learn much, though, because it was too damned fast!"[6] Smith joined various groups, but found his musical surroundings holding him back, so decided to go it alone. Babs Gonzales, who wrote the sleeve notes for *A New Sound, A New Star*, mentions going to see Smith live in 1955 and being amazed at the 40 choruses of inventive soloing he played on one tune, and the "futuristic stratospheric sounds that were never before explored on the organ".

A New Sound, A New Star, Smith's debut for the Blue Note label, featured the classic organ trio line-up of guitarist Thornel Schwartz and drummer Bay Perry. Rudy Van Gelder was the engineer and the album included a mix of standards and originals about to become standards, such as 'You Get'cha' from Smith himself and 'The Preacher' by the influential Horace Silver. The record made a huge impact in terms of both sound and content. Interestingly though, if you listen to 'The Way You Look Tonight', or 'Lady Be Good', the swing and melodic feel are all there, but the sound, which includes some upper partials in the comping (chordal accompaniment) and the soloing, isn't as groovy as the classic drawbar setting he was to make his own.

Word gets around though, and just a year later, Smith was able to assemble a band of top musicians to appear on *Jimmy Smith At The Organ*: Kenny Burrell on guitar, Lou Donaldson on alto sax, and Blue Note stablemate Art Blakey on drums. Blakey's band, The Jazz Messengers, had just stopped working with the ubiquitous

WILD BILL DAVIS TOLD JIMMY SMITH IT WOULD TAKE HIM TEN YEARS JUST TO LEARN THE PEDALS. BUT THAT ONLY INCREASED HIS RESOLVE TO MASTER THE INSTRUMENT.

Horace Silver, and here he propels the quartet on Charlie Parker's 'Yardbird Suite' with customary exuberance. Smith's sound has settled by now. It has lost any trace of theatre or schmaltz, and picked up Silver's 'funk' and drive. Skipping forward a year to *The Sermon!*, probably Jimmy Smith's best-known record for Blue Note, the elements are all in place. With 16 albums under his belt already, it's time to stretch out on an original, and that means a single track on one side of the album, lasting 20:12. The tune is 'The Sermon', dedicated to Horace Silver.

It's a great band: Burrell, Blakey, and Donaldson, plus Lee Morgan on trumpet and Tina Brooks on tenor. To last the course it needs to be. Kicking off with the 'soul-jazz' coolness of a waving palm leaf on a summer's day, the feel is relaxed and expectant, the composer in trio mode on the opening choruses and solo. It doesn't take long for a stuttering F to appear, a trademark repeated-note motif, and the choruses gradually edge their way into a mid-tempo groove without too much excitement.

Soundwise, it's time to reveal the not-so-secret secret that is the Jimmy Smith lead-line drawbar setting. Of course there's no such thing as always, but mostly it's 888000000, the first three drawbars full out with percussion on, fast decay, soft volume, and vibrato set to C3. When it comes to the question of second or third harmonic percussion, the oracle will tell you that default for Jimmy Smith is third, but on 'The Sermon' the third doesn't quite match up and my vote would be that he used second. On the head, the main theme, he's playing left-hand bass on the

lower manual and right-hand tune/solo on the upper. Touches of volume pedal are around when needed, but to nothing like the extent of Wild Bill Davis and others of the 'theatre school'. A few choruses in, Smith's knowledge of tunes is to the fore as he quotes what was then a recent song, Gene De Paul and Sammy Cahn's 'Teach Me Tonight' of 1953. See **Sound And Style 1, p121, CD track 17**.

The baton is passed from solo to solo, and the pace quickens considerably into a raucous brass shout before the organ leads into a fade. If you'd had the vinyl, side two would have contained the lively 'J.O.S.' (James Oscar Smith, say the sleeve notes), and 'Flamingo', an achingly poignant version that features Lee Morgan and Kenny Burrell. Smith himself lays down, according to the sleeve notes, "a deep pile carpet to walk on, a perfectly heated pool to swim in, an adequately logged fireplace ..."

If Smith takes a back seat on 'J.O.S.', the opposite is true on the well-known 'Back At The Chicken Shack', from the album of the same name, recorded in 1960 with Burrell, Donald Bailey on drums, and the tenor sax player Stanley Turrentine. The longest solo is his, and he relishes the space. Bailey is interesting; drier and occasionally funkier, his input seems to push the group sound further into soul-jazz.

If the Blue Note years were about breakthrough in both musical and music business terms, the Verve years were based on consolidating that success and expanding into a big-band line-up. Some say – and critics at the time certainly said – that tending to commerce diluted the jazz. Nevertheless, some of Jimmy Smith's Verve tracks, particularly with Oliver Nelson on board, are his best known. Verve went straight for the jugular with the first album, *Bashin': The Unpredictable Jimmy Smith*, hiring Nelson as arranger and conductor of a big band featuring, among many others, the alto saxophonist Phil Woods. Recorded at the end of March 1962, with Creed Taylor producing and Rudy Van Gelder still on board, 'Walk On The Wild Side', a quick 3/4 blues, finds Smith sounding constricted as a player amidst the huge band texture, but the piece as a whole is exciting enough. The 'stutter' trademark is elaborated by leaping out of the single-note reiteration to other notes, and the whole piece ends with a classic Jimmy Smith F-blues run-down that seems to contain his whole world in microcosm.

The organ sound is closer and more detailed than in the Blue Note regime; different producer, different ears. Three more big-band tracks make up side one, but side two is back to the trio format. Smith's own tune, 'Bashin'', stands out here. Almost a fully-fledged soul number, with a slightly over-insistent snare on beat four, it lets Smith take his time; and the theme includes a tasteful two-against-three

Brother Jack McDuff: starting out on bass, McDuff switched to Hammond at the behest of bandleader Willis Jackson.

chromatic falling line that he finds hard to leave alone for all the right reasons.

Then of course there's *The Cat*, released in 1964. Argentinian Lalo Schifrin wrote tunes, arranged for big band, conducted, and generally displayed an overdose of talent. On 'The Cat' itself, Smith is given time after an initial shout to get heavily involved with a particularly 1960s groovy rhythm track, with Grady Tate on drums. The tangling continues and intensifies at the solo climax but there's never any doubt as to who's in charge, with Smith in domineering form. Nice arranging touches too, guitar and marimba doubling the part in the 'outhead', when the opening tune is restated. The arrangement is to the fore on Elmer Bernstein's 'The Carpetbaggers': 9/8 groove, brass fully extended, French horns over-extended but splendid, and a Jimmy Smith who sounds like he's having a ball exploring a highly original feel.

The same sense of enjoyment pervades 'Got My Mojo Workin'', from the album of the same name, recorded in 1965. The unashamedly showy, repetitive solo licks are perfectly executed, and there's the bonus of Smith's earthy, soul-blues singing.

Of the other Verve records, the Jimmy Smith and Wes Montgomery album, *The Dynamic Duo*, shows two players at the height of their powers. On 'James And Wes', Smith is particularly blistering, the tempo just meshing with his high-speed 16th-note outbursts. Egging each other on isn't quite it, nor is competitive; it's more a question of mutual inspiration and having the ability to act on it.

> 'THE BEST JAZZ, BLUES, BEBOP, FUNK, IT'S AN EXPRESSION OF SEX,' SMITH ONCE SAID. 'THE MUSIC IS NOTHING WITHOUT THAT ENERGY. NOW YOU KNOW.'

So it continued, for another 40 years, until Jimmy Smith's death in 2005. He had been working with Joey DeFrancesco on a couple of albums involving two B-3s and some new slants on old tunes, released as *Incredible* and *Legacy* on the Concord label. To have recorded so much music is one thing, to keep on doing it is another. Where did the energy come from? "The best jazz, blues, bebop, funk, it's an expression of sex," Smith once said. "You can't say out loud what you wanna do, but you can say it with the instrument. The music is nothing without that energy. Now you know."[7]

It's controversial to talk about the post-Smith school of jazz organists, but it is a way of defining, chronologically at least, a line of those joining the Hammond party. They all had their own distinguishing marks, but Brother Jack McDuff probably had the most sophisticated jazz technique and musical language. What he lacked was the earthy yet nimble bravado and funk of Richard 'Groove' Holmes, and the intense blues/gospel leanings of the commercially astute Jimmy McGriff.

Born in 1926 as Eugene McDuffy, Brother Jack McDuff started his musical life by teaching himself piano and organ, but his first gig was as a bass player with the likes of jazz composer Danny Zeitlin (who also wrote the score for *Invasion Of The Body Snatchers*) on piano and Joe Farrell on saxes. Heavy company, but that seemed to be the way with McDuff. He could pick a band, and had a particularly keen instinct for guitarists; he would later work with Pat Martino and George Benson.

Switching to piano, McDuff led his own bands before sliding over to the Hammond at the behest of bandleader Willis Jackson. Jackson's record company, Prestige, soon showed an interest in McDuff and a string of albums followed from 1960 onwards. The line-ups mostly including bass players, but when McDuff took care of bass business himself it was to great effect. *Tough Duff*, released in 1960, featured organ, vibes, tenor, and drums, but the real deal seems to be the next album. Recorded in February 1961, *The Honeydripper* featured Jimmy Forrest on tenor sax, Ben Dixon on drums, and newcomer guitarist Grant Green, who shows not a hint of intimidation.

First up on *The Honeydripper* is 'Whap', a McDuff original that harks back to bebop while also managing to look forward to the late 1990s collaborations between saxophonist Michael Brecker and organist Larry Goldings. 'Whap' shows McDuff to be no slouch in either the arranging or playing stakes. With the tune played in harmony between organ and sax so as you hardly know where the tune lies, McDuff's solo builds from simple to punchy, using a drawbar combination on the top manual that cuts through effectively. It's something resembling 888840000 with normal/fast/third-harmonic percussion. The group feel, with an elegant and propulsive bass line, is exemplary, with Green slotting in between bass and lead as if McDuff possessed another limb. The content isn't extraordinary until after the sax solo, when a trading of four bars each from organ and sax gives way to complex harmonic layering, in which phrases are played in a superimposed unrelated key. Then things get back on track for the slightly overdriven guitar solo, to which engineer Rudy Van Gelder adds reverb.

Henry Mancini had a hit single with 'Mr Lucky', the name of a popular TV show at the time, using Hammond as a featured instrument, which planted in the public consciousness the idea that organs were cool and sophisticated, Cary Grant-ish instruments. McDuff's version contrasts a full, sax-supporting top manual with a subtler fundamental lower keyboard. The top drawbar setting, 858800553, includes a smattering of top for that extra sparkling sizzle. The most extraordinary

Jimmy McGriff: blues was what he did, right from the off.

sound though, is to be found not on the groovy 'The Honeydripper', nor on the two blues tracks, but on the other ballad from the set, 'I Want A Little Girl'. The tune is voiced with parallel thirds, provoking an extreme Leslie shimmer that's 'out there': 840000088 was the closest I could get. **Sound And Style 2, p122, CD track 18.**

McDuff was apparently concerned that he'd included too much of the blues on *The Honeydripper*, but looking at the album from here that's not the case. Jimmy McGriff, on the other hand, might have been accused of a surfeit of blues, but blues was what he did, right from the off. Born in 1936 in the organ hotbed of Philadelphia, he came from a family that was marinated in music. Both his parents played piano, as did Smith's, and he had two cousins with musical leanings, the saxophonist/writer Benny Golson ('Whisper Not', 'Killer Joe') and the singer Harold Melvin, famous for his hit with The Blue Notes, 'If You Don't Know Me By Now'. No instrument was too hard for young James. Drums, bass, alto sax, vibes, piano: you name it, he played it. Having taken some initial instruction on Hammond from Richard 'Groove' Holmes, McGriff joined the police force before returning to music on bass. Later her returned to Holmes for lessons, then attended the Juilliard School in New York City, while receiving private organ tuition from first Milt Buckner and then Jimmy Smith. Not a bad selection of teachers, you might say.

Then came the hit. His version of Ray Charles's 'I've Got A Woman', released in 1963, went Top Five in the rhythm & blues chart and nearly reached the Top 20 in the pop singles chart. Many would say he never bettered his debut album; and with three singles pulled from it, the record company, Sue, must have been delighted. 'I've Got A Woman' is an urgent 12/8 shuffle, which reflects the current rock and roll phase, as does the next single, 'All About My Girl', even if the tempo is more staid. The production has a good helping of dirt thrown in, which seems to be a McGriff distinction.

They say every Hammond has its own personality and there's a metallic edge to McGriff's organ sound, whether it's in the instrument or the production. He's not afraid of a dusting of reverb, either. By the time of his move to Solid State records in 1966, the music is verging on jazz fusion. *The Worm*, from 1969, is a fully paid-up member of that society. A two-chord vamp, underpinned by electric bass, is all that is required to keep things simmering on the title track, which features Grady Tate on drums. The organ is pretty much at a rhythm section level and doesn't quite shine, even on the solo. **Sound And Style 3, p123, CD track 19.**

Producer Sonny Lester never quite manages to pull the listener inside the picture, but the playing is good. First and second solos go to octave-divided sax, then Blue Mitchell's trumpet, and then Jimmy piles in with a short burst of something in the region of 888800000. But then horns are in again and the track is on the fade.

To catch McGriff in full flight, you might prefer a live album, and where better than playing dual B-3s with his inspiration, Richard 'Groove' Holmes. Five years older than McGriff, Holmes was the genuine article. Many of the organists mentioned so far played bass lines with their left hand on the lower manual. Pedals would be called upon in ballads and slower swing tunes. Nothing wrong with that. In fact, Jimmy Smith went one stage further, by either doubling the left hand with pedals or just marking each beat on his note of choice, a thudding B that had more in common with a bass drum than the note itself. That effect, coupled with a skip in the left hand, gave him his very individual swing feel. Holmes, however, was fluent with his feet, capable of supplying three interesting arenas of action simultaneously. Most of us have a problem with one, two is a challenge, and three a circus act. But it's possible: look at Barbara Dennerlein and Mike Carr.

The concert dates that McGriff and Holmes set up in the early 1970s must have been completely earth-shattering; on stage there would have been two B-3s and their Leslies, two guitarists (presumably each organist had his favourite comping/soloing partner), a drummer, and to top it all off, a fashionable percussionist. For *Giants Of The Organ In Concert*, Sonny Lester recorded a gig of original tunes live at Paul's Mall in Boston in 1973, capturing some of the excitement of the occasion. If you are not a Hammond enthusiast it's quite full on, there being no horns to supply a timbral break, but in short spurts it's very entertaining indeed. What instantly grabs you is the stylistic proximity between the two players. Each is capable of long passages of 16th-note action, and you have to keep reminding yourself who's who. The last track, 'Chopper', finds them in blues mode, with Holmes employing his secret weapon, the 1' drawbar. Using Jimmy Smith's solo setting plus 1' (888000008), his solos whistle along like a pensioner with a gap in his teeth.

Turning attention fully to Holmes, he recorded his first album by tagging on to the end of a Les McCann vocal session. The musicians were so enamoured with each other that they immediately decided to record as a unit instrumentally, which is how legend Ben Webster turns up on *Groove*, Holmes' 1961 debut for the label Pacific Jazz. Pacific was to stand him in pretty good stead; in a four-year stint he made seven albums, the last including the medium-tempo version of 'Misty' that brought him to a huge audience. On 'Groovin' Time', from *Welcome Home* in 1968, hard bop is to the fore, with tenor sax player Teddy Edwards providing the arrangements and a veritable A-list band including horn players Tom Scott, Wilton

Felder, and Chuck Finley. A pulsing blues is passing by at 240 beats per minute, just short of the speed of sound. Holmes takes several choruses with customary 1' tickling and mostly eighth-note action when suddenly a whole bunch of 16th-notes appear from nowhere; the speed and articulation are simply scary.

Other instances of brilliance abound. A simple descending swing bassline, given jugloads of feel on 'Morris The Minor', from *Groovin' With Jug*; the intro to 'Old Folks', from *Spicy*, where drawbar manipulation injects some adrenalin into the top manual while Holmes is glissing up and down the lower manual, making it sound remarkably like a bell tree; the whole of '(Back Home Again In) Indiana', from the album *On Basie's Bandstand* (recorded in 1966, released in 2003), which is a showcase for just about everything, even if the rhythm section is a little creaky at times.

It has been argued that Holmes never quite got to play with the best players, and there is some validity to that. His choice of material can be iffy too; it's best to leave Latin to the Latins. Incidentally, several times on record he manages to hold a chord and then 'bend' it as if he had a pitch-bend wheel; something he achieved with turning on and off, I suspect. He also has a perverse anti-emotional habit of removing fast Leslie where most players add it. Strangely, this begins to work after a while, the nakedness of the sound provoking a musical tension and slight discomfort that is completely anti-cheese. One more thing: he carried his B-3 around in a second-hand Cadillac hearse. **Sound And Style 4, p124, CD track 20.**

It seems churlish to cover the other participants of the jazz soul explosion in a few sentences; fine Hammond players all, they belong in the pantheon of greats. Philly-born Charles Earland came through as a tenor sax player in McGriff's band, then became fascinated by the Hammond. His bass lines were legendary, and recording for Prestige, he managed to hire the aspiring saxophonist Grover Washington Jr. Don Patterson had a great jazz (bebop) feel; laid-back and melodically inventive, he seems to eschew the theatrical, which is probably what attracted sax-player Sonny Stitt to his playing. *Legends Of Acid Jazz* features Patterson alongside tenor player Booker Ervin. Bill Doggett, yet another Philly native, worked as a sideman with The Ink Spots, then replaced Wild Bill Davis in Louis Jordan's band, then had a huge rock'n'roll hit with 'Honky Tonk' in 1956; and all the while he was happier playing blues and gospel organ on the club scene.

Without a doubt 1955-65 was a great decade for the Hammond. Not only did the organ find a true niche in the world of jazz, it contributed to the development of that music by bringing in other flavours, sourced from a variety of skilled (and schooled, mostly) musicians. Meanwhile other American players were straying from the Smith model, widening the musical contexts of Hammond playing.

The jazz soul funk brothers and sisters

No-one is quite sure why Dr Lonnie Smith calls himself 'Dr', or why he wears a turban, but these idiosyncracies have succeeded in making the man something of an enigma. Raised in Buffalo, New York, he was a teenage singer who hung around a music shop until the owner presented him with a B-3, which he taught himself to play; or at least, that's how the story goes. Put that together with being asked to do a Grant Green session as if from nowhere, and you have a slice of history.

Modesty kept him from doing that session, but when George Benson came calling, Smith was ready; the pair formed the George Benson quartet in 1966. A year later, Smith recorded his first solo album, *Finger Lickin' Good*, a funk workout ahead of its time, for Columbia. Then Blue Note signed him. The result was 1968's *Think!*, which is a joy in its 2005 24-bit Van Gelder re-mastering. The soul groove 'Slouchin'' finds Smith discreetly accompanying David 'Fathead' Newman (sax) and Lee Morgan (trumpet), before taking the limelight with a curate's egg of a solo. The lines unfold gradually, with his drawbars set to 888800000, and then he starts cascading a whole series of Gm7/C7 licks before appearing to lose his thread all together and being rescued by the horns when they restate the tune at the end. But the writing is adventurous. Another number, 'Call Of The Wild', contains a brass and organ chorale that goes beyond the normal limits of soul jazz.

So too does Smith's next album, 1969's *Turning Point*, an adventure in the company of two future Herbie Hancock sidemen, Julian Priester (trombone) and Benny Maupin (reeds). *Drives*, released in 1970, takes an altogether funkier direction. The track called 'Psychedelic Pi' is of its time, but its use of fourth chords is interesting, plus it's the first instance I have found of doubling falsetto voice and organ. Smith is a man who divides opinion, but there's a real charm behind the music as well as an inquiring mind. **Sound And Style 5, p125, CD track 21.**

No-one could accuse Shirley Scott of being out there and beyond. She brings a keen sense of economy to the music. No floral, baroque, over-decorated licks for her; she just plays the tune, and very well too. Real artistry lies behind the 1960s gloss. She's another Philly resident who kept very good company. While very young she would play piano with a young John Coltrane, before joining forces with Eddie 'Lockjaw' Davis, the tenor player. They recorded for Prestige, and the general sound and feel have a lightness about them, with the organ missing out the 16' drawbar. Her decade was the 1960s. Scott was married to saxophonist Stanley Turrentine through to the early 1970s, and their collaborations, with the assistance of the likes of arranger Oliver Nelson, bassist George Duvivier and

Dr Lonnie Smith: something of an enigma.

Shirley Scott: real artistry behind the 1960s gloss.

visitors such as Clark Terry (trumpet) and Ron Carter (bass), were among her most ambitious recordings. *Great Scott*, released on the Impulse label in 1964, showcases a Henry Mancini tune, 'A Shot In The Dark', using a typically 1960s big band and a percussion setting that serves beautifully to articulate the tune.

The percussion setting on the top manual works like a single-trigger synth; you have to release the key to spark off the percussion on the next note. Play legato, however, and the notes have no percussion, giving the player more phrase-shaping options. Shirley Scott uses the effect to maximum advantage. (Just one more peculiarity concerning percussion: it disables the 1' drawbar, so all those whistling Richard 'Groove' Holmes solos have none.) **Sound And Style 6, p126, CD track 22.**

'Heat Wave', on the 1966 album *Soul Duo*, has to be my number one choice of Scott material. Clark Terry, the other half of the duo, plays fine trumpet, and Scott responds with a solo that's airy yet still digs deep. She had a bad time with her heart, courtesy of the prescription drug Fen-Phen, and died in 2002. Heart problems seem to have accounted for more than a few of the top-flight organists, including Holmes in 1991 and McDuff in 2001.

Larry Young's career ended prematurely, but not through heart problems. He died in 1978, at the age of 38, from untreated pneumonia. Before that he had dragged his Hammond, kicking and screaming, from the soul jazz suburbs into the fusion city centre. Starting out as a Jimmy Smith disciple, Young broke away from the blues-based enclave and struck out in a direction that reflected more of the changes going on in the steaming cauldron of jazz. On the way he passed through modal improvisation, then almost free improvisation in the company of the extraordinary Tony Williams (drums) and John McLaughlin (guitar).

SHIRLEY SCOTT BRINGS A KEEN SENSE OF ECONOMY TO THE MUSIC. NO FLORAL, BAROQUE, OVER-DECORATED LICKS FOR HER. SHE JUST PLAYS THE TUNE, AND VERY WELL.

Electricity was powering up jazz in a big way. Hammonds and guitar amps were powerful enough, but as nothing compared to the sound manipulation technology and electric instruments waiting in the pipeline. Miles Davis's 1969 record, *Bitches Brew*, employed both electric and acoustic basses and at least two electric pianos, and the whole was manipulated by producer Teo Macero, using tape loops, reverberation, and tape editing. Who was sitting in the midst of this, in between either Joe Zawinul or Herbie Hancock and Chick Corea? None other than Larry Young, contributing Rhodes and celeste.

But let's back up a bit. It's November 10th 1965, Blue Note is recording Larry Young's *Unity*, and the band is first rate; Woody Shaw (trumpet), Joe Henderson (tenor), and drummer Elvin Jones, who was approaching the end of the line with John Coltrane. All four are at the top of their game; there is indeed a unity of purpose. Young is in the Jimmy Smith drawbar ballpark, (888800000, percussion soft), but the soloing is informed by wider influences, particularly in his use of three-note ascending fourths phrases. By the way, there's no evidence of pedals; it sounds like left-hand bass all the way. **Sound And Style 7, p128, CD track 23.**

'Softly, As In A Morning Sunrise' and 'Beyond All Limits', a Woody Shaw tune of some complexity, test Young to the limits. Soloing, he can stumble, but the power of Jones's drumming picks him up. The music has weathered well, sound and content perfectly in place.

Then, in 1969, Tony Williams and his group Lifetime recorded *Emergency!*, an album that sent crashing waves against the jazz cliffs. This one has not lasted so well, but you can't imagine a world without it. The Hammond is treated and reverbed, and in all the playing assumes more of a group textural role. Young is occasionally reduced to supporting artist by the ferocious McLaughlin, but it marks the point of no return for him; after that experience the avant garde would beckon. It is good that Young's output post-*Lifetime* would continue to be interesting; not so good the way it would be prematurely ended.

Jimmy Smith's soul jazz legacy had led Young to the jazz avant garde, but it led others down other paths, notably into funk. Down in New Orleans, Art Neville formed a band called The Meters: the use of a band name, rather than those of individuals, is one mark of the transition. Neville co-wrote the band's seminal funk tune 'Cissy Strut', later recorded by guitarist John Scofield and keyboard player John Medeski, and was central to the band's mix of riff-based guitar and organ. From an organ point of view, the hit 'Sophisticated Cissy' is the track to listen to from their debut album *The Meters*. It sports a slow funk groove, guitar in blues/funk style and a full Hammond sound in the region of top manual 888808000, percussion on soft, fast, second harmonic. The lower manual is pressed into service for the bridge, 008000008, but it's the opening glissando up to a held top C and B-flat that raises the heartbeat. Use of that top octave with intervals of seconds and thirds is about to become a call sign: the rock/funk/blues generation has arrived.

"You might want to hear my organ!" is another rallying cry, clearly enunciated

Art Neville (top); Booker T. Jones with The MGs (bottom right); Sly & The Family Stone (bottom left).

by Sly Stone on 'Dance To The Music', from the 1967 Sly & The Family Stone album of the same name. What we hear is a very fine break, choppy and with funky two-hander chords from a pretty full-on Hammond. 'Stand', from the 1969 album of the same name, is pushing along very nicely until a new plateau is reached and in comes the Hammond, firing on all two manuals. There's a pattern building here. A moment of climax? Call for the organ. A Hammond can be just as happy sitting in an arrangement as being at the forefront of the action. Listen to Sly & The Family Stone's 'Everybody Is A Star', a single from 1969. The organ features at the front end then slides back comfortably into the ensemble. Sly Stone was an occasional Hammond player. He also played other keyboards, including the clavinet, and he was an ace guitarist into the bargain.

Another racially integrated line-up had been working as house band for the Stax record label in Memphis since the early 1960s. Steve Cropper on guitar, bassist Lewie Steinberg (later replaced by Donald 'Duck' Dunn), drummer Al Jackson Jr., and organist and multi-instrumentalist Booker T. Jones had turned out tracks for the Stax roster, backing Wilson Pickett, The Staple Singers, Otis Redding, and Albert King, among others. Mention Hammond organ to a man or woman in the street and the first response will likely be Jimmy Smith, but the second will more often than not be Booker T. & The MGs. The track, of course, is 'Green Onions', from 1962, and very slinky it is too. It was the result of dead time in the studio, waiting for a singer named Billy Lee Riley to turn up for a session. The resulting riff has the immediacy of a 'Watermelon Man' or a 'Canteloupe Island', both Herbie Hancock tunes, both in the 'Onions' key of F minor. Clearly the mid-tempo F minor sound was swimming around in the consciousness at that time.

It's hard to position 'Green Onions' on the scale of blues to funk; put up against The Meters it gets firmly pushed to the blues end of the spectrum on the grounds of the simplicity of its shuffle groove, which is precisely why it's so infectious, up there with Neal Hefti's 'Batman'. Some of the *Green Onions* album does come over as 1960s history to modern ears, 'Rinky Dink' and 'One Who Really Loves You' being the main poppy offenders; and perhaps 'Stranger On The Shore' should have been left to Acker Bilk and 'Twist and Shout' to The Beatles. But the rest are couched in a bluesy ambience that has retained its honesty through the decades. There's nothing wrong with the recording either. Again, it's an honest and fair representation of four people playing, with very few tricks up its sleeve, which means that you can really hear the organ.

What's immediately apparent is that Booker T. is not a tricksy man when it comes to sound choices. Over the album there's a wide variety of registrations, but as he says, "Ever since I began playing the organ as a boy, I've been mainly enticed by the straight sound. That's the real beauty of the Hammond, and that's still how I like to hear it today."[8] He's not a great user of either percussion or Leslie; sometimes the sound is uncomfortable in its state of undress, but mostly the quality of playing is adequate compensation.

'Green Onions' itself starts with that vamp on lower keyboard. The key to it is the rocking off the left hand, anticipating the downbeat with a C then later in the bar an F. In much the same way that Donald Fagen of Steely Dan can set the entirety of a groove by playing the first four bars, Booker T.'s vamp contains the germ of the whole track, couched in a drawbar setting of 008808000. With the entry of the melody on the top manual the setting resembles 888800000, with no percussion. **Sound And Style 8, p130, CD track 24.**

These days one might be worried about Booker T.'s extreme dotted-note solo rhythm style. The prevailing fashion is for a looser triplet swing groove, but the feel here is very much part of the character and charm of the piece, which helps to make the track not only of its time but before its time.

Before leaving the soul and funk area there are a couple of honourable mentions to be made. In the interest of sexual equality, one is Rhoda Scott; the other is Bernie Worrell. Scott was the daughter of a preacher, raised at the Hammond. By the age of seven she could find her way around the organ. She studied in Manhattan, then followed in the footsteps of Quincy Jones by travelling to Paris, France, to study with the legendary teacher Nadia Boulanger. Alternating between New York City and Paris, she has carved a name for herself as an intelligent and musical jazzer. Her 1977 record with drummer Kenny Clarke finds her particularly colourful and expressive on ballads. She is not afraid to use the complete range of drawbars and Leslie, and makes careful and effective use of the volume pedal to extract every ounce of angst from 'It's Impossible' and 'What Are You Doing The Rest Of Your Life?' A pedal player, she became known as the 'barefoot organist', for obvious reasons.

Funk stylist Bernie Worrell has been keyboardist and sideman to several greats, most notably George Clinton, David Byrne, and Bill Laswell. Hammond is just one side of his armoury – he pioneered Minimoog basslines in the 1970s – but when he pulls out the drawbars it's for a good reason. He started out on organ, playing in the house band at Basin Street South, a club in Boston, backing people like Dionne Warwick and Tammi Terrell.

FOLLOWING PAGE **Booker T. Jones (main picture); Rhoda Scott (top right); Bernie Worrell (bottom right).**

For an original take on contemporary organ, check out the intriguing 'Set The Tone/Victory', from his 1993 album *Pieces Of Woo: The Other Side*, which sets churchy tones against synth squelch against intoned poetry. With Worrell being such a well armed keyboardist, and the track being recent, we enter into the realm of uncertainty as to the authenticity of organ tracks. Samples and clones and virtual models have progressed to the point where it's occasionally impossible to spot an imitation. But I don't think you could produce 'At Mos' Spheres', from his 1990 album *Funk Of Ages*, without the authentic instrument. Churchy and contrapuntal, gospel-tinged and even melodramatic, it still has the power to move, with a perfect demonstration of Leslie technique for the climax, and an illustration of how good the top drawbars sound when treated further through a phaser.

Strange isn't it, how the influence of the church on the Hammond's beginnings refuses to go away, how plagal cadences lend a tone of seriousness (albeit sometimes ironically), and how the B-3 is still very much part of the fabric of the modern church scene? Much great music has come almost straight out of church into the concert hall, as have many fine musicians.

The gospel tradition

It can be no coincidence that the invention and development of the tonewheel organ matches exactly the period in which gospel music was recognised, grew into a popular style, and then moved away from the church and into a secular world ready to embrace it. Whether or not one's personal beliefs lie that way, it's still possible to feel the inherent strength of emotion in gospel music in the same way as Bach's 'St Matthew Passion' can move non-believers. Many of the organists who regularly play in churches never come to the attention of a wider public, but occasionally a musician manages both to keep the faith and to leap into the dangerous waters of the music business. One such player was Billy Preston.

Gospel is the result of an exchange of influences between church and secular musics. The forms that developed through the 19th century came from the mixing of African rhythmic and vocal ideas with western harmony. These forms include the spiritual and the 'call and response' tradition, as perfectly illustrated in Ray Charles's 'What'd I Say'. By the beginning of the 20th century, the blues tradition was influencing the sound of church music, and soon ragtime and other jazz styles were working their way into church. What's more, the piano was often the first choice for accompaniment, so the gospel style evolved in the natural company of keyboards. Thomas A. Dorsey, the man credited with coining the term 'gospel', was a blues pianist before turning to sacred music; the lyrics had changed but the sound remained the same.

Mahalia Jackson was the first crossover gospel artist, possessing one of the most incredible voices ever to have inhabited the planet. She sang from an early age, both solo and in choirs in the Baptist church, blending the blues of Bessie Smith with the Baptist tradition. Her career was slow to build. She recorded first for Decca, in 1937, but continued to perform and 'invoke the spirit' in church. The big time finally beckoned in 1948 with the release of 'Move On Up A Little Higher', on the Apollo label; it would go on to sell eight million copies.

By this time the Hammond was fully ensconced next to the piano, bass guitar, and drums in Mahalia's backing group. In the 1950s, Lilton Mitchell and Ralph Jones were among the names to be found on the organ seat, but guess who would appear on a 1963 recording, alongside jazz names Shelley Manne on drums and Herb Ellis on guitar? It was a young man used to the limelight: Billy Preston. On tracks including 'Walk In Jerusalem' and 'He Calmed The Ocean', he is not featured as a soloist but is very certainly comfortable grooving. A mere 17 years old, Preston had already tasted stardom by playing bluesman W.C. Handy as a boy in the 1958 movie 'St Louis Blues'. As part of the publicity, he had appeared on the Nat 'King' Cole's TV show at the age of 12, confidently swapping seats with Cole for alternate verses of 'Blueberry Hill', playing Hammond and singing like a bird.

OCCASIONALLY A MUSICIAN MANAGES BOTH TO KEEP THE FAITH AND TO LEAP INTO THE DANGEROUS WATERS OF THE MUSIC BUSINESS. ONE SUCH PLAYER WAS BILLY PRESTON.

Preston would tour with Jackson, Little Richard, and Ray Charles, and in 1965 made his own album, *The Most Exciting Organ Ever*, on VJ records. Ambitious marketing, and it can't be said that the album lives up to its title, but he was 19 and this was his first album, so who's complaining? With the Hammond augmented by piano, guitar, bass, drums, and percussion, the soul jazz, blues gospel strains are evident in the playing, and the influence of Booker T. in some of the writing. 'Billy's Bag', an original tune, is a mid-tempo stomp on a loose blues form. The Hammond is pretty much full on, and much changing of presets, much Leslie engaging and dis-engaging, and many glissandi never quite compensate for the lack of quality compositional input.

Billy Preston: a phenomenal Hammond player in the gospel tradition.

What happened next is well known. Preston had met The Beatles in 1962 while on tour with Little Richard. In 1969, George Harrison had walked out of the fractious *Let It Be* sessions and gone to a Ray Charles gig in London. There he renewed his acquaintance with Preston and invited him back to the studio, where his musicianship and amenable personality defused some of the tension. It led to 'Get Back', one of the singles from the sessions, being credited to 'The Beatles with Billy Preston'. He solos on electric piano on that track, but on 'Let It Be' he gets a crack at the organ, a challenge he responds to with selfless restraint, laying down a pad for much of the latter part of the track, but with an organ 'moment' before the guitar solo. (An approximation would be 888004440, no percussion, no vibrato, fast Leslie.) The 'Naked' mix, without choirs and Phil Spector's sweetenings, shows Preston's contribution in a far clearer light.

Where do you go from there, having enjoyed such success at such a young age? Preston managed to expand his career by writing and recording *That's The Way God Planned It* for the Apple label in 1969. The heavyweights on that album included Keith Richards on bass, Eric Clapton and George Harrison on guitars, and Ginger Baker on drums. The next outing on Apple was, if anything, more interesting. *Encouraging Words*, from 1970, has gospel versions of two Harrison songs, 'My Sweet Lord' and 'Everything Must Pass', and a funky take on The Beatles' 'I've Got A Feeling'. Busy can hardly begin to describe Preston's life post-Apple; tours and sessions with The Rolling Stones, Syreeta Wright, Eric Clapton, and more albums of his own. To pick a few organ highlights, 'Outa-Space', from his 1971 album *I Wrote A Simple Song*, pits the Hammond against the Clavinet, another instrument of which Preston was the master. 'Space Race', from 1973's *Everybody Likes Some Kind Of Music*, draws on Hammond, Clavinet, and Minimoog, just about as fresh and contemporary a combination as you can find.

It has to be said that Preston milked his previous connections for every last drop, and the Beatles covers are not his best work by any means. He was a phenomenal Hammond user; but that wasn't all he was using to fuel his hectic lifestyle. Alcohol and drugs served to scupper his career; he released no albums between 1985 and 1995. The cocaine lifestyle left its damaging mark, and at one point he was convicted for setting fire to his LA house and claiming the insurance: at the time of the trial he was already in prison for violating probation on a conviction for possession of cocaine. It seems true to say that he never conquered his addictions, but he continued to work when he could. A year after the death of George Harrison, Preston hooked up with Clapton to put on the Concert For George in 2002. He played Hammond throughout and sang a great version of 'My

Sweet Lord'. In later years he battled with kidney disease. A transplant in 2002 failed to halt his decline and he died in 2006 after spending seven months in a coma.

Preston was a keyboard player in the broadest of senses, but starting on the Hammond did pay dividends. For a definition of gospel Hammond-style, go to Preston's version of the American hymn 'How Great Thou Art'. Leave aside your preconceptions and doubts concerning religious fervour and listen to that track – or watch the video version, which can be found, at the time of writing, on YouTube. It's recorded in 1988, live in church, and spontaneous applause breaks out at every dramatic turn or high held note dragged back by the volume pedal. Drawbar settings change from theatrical, to pure, to ghostly, while diminished chord harmony racks up the tension. As for glissandi, there's every variation: ghostly space capsules taking off, left hand glisses under the full held chord, and glissing with both palms then thinning out to one note only. 'How Great Thou Art' is an absolute physical, technical, and emotional tour de force, and as near to Hammond ecstasy as it's possible to record. **Sound And Style 9, p132, CD track 25.**

Rhythm & blues and the B

By the early 1960s, the rhythm & blues scene was rumbling in the UK, particularly in London. Interest in the blues of Robert Johnson was fuelling a wave of bands that initially re-created the blues but soon found improvisational routes away from the basic formula. Many of the bandleaders had keyboard skills, and how better to display them than by running up and down Hammond keys? If Philadelphia was the USA's organ city, then London was its trans-Atlantic cousin, and the Hammond became almost obligatory in many of the blues bands' line-ups. Most of the players were strong characters, with an air of confidence bordering on arrogance and a flamboyance that saw them re-exporting the music worldwide.

One of these larger-than-life types was Graham Bond, originally a pianist and then an alto saxophonist who had paid his dues in commercial dance bands. Unfortunately, he began to frighten the punters with the hard edge of his playing style, so he had to occasionally augment his income by selling refridgerators. In 1960, he began working with fellow saxophonist Dick Heckstall-Smith. A year later he joined another saxophonist, Don Rendell, to form the Don Rendell quintet.

Jazz work flowed in, but Bond was eager to return to playing piano, so he joined one of the hothouses of British rhythm & blues, Alexis Korner's Blues Incorporated. Charlie Watts had just vacated the drum seat, to be replaced by

Graham Bond: larger than life.

Ginger Baker, and Jack Bruce was on bass. At this point Bond took up the organ, playing in a trio with Bruce and Baker. Georgie Fame saw him and was inspired to take up the Hammond.

In February 1965, Bond had this to say to the *Melody Maker* : "Two years ago I was one of the first to play organ. In that two years the organ and tenor sound has spread.... We use the organ far more than most groups that feature it, because we are a smaller group.

"The organ is a logical progression from the big band sound, which died the death. It gets the same wide variety of sounds. The organ gets a jerky, unswinging effect if it is played in a piano style. I took piano lessons, but I know I don't play organ like a piano and never have done. Hands have to be flatter than raised as they are for the piano, because it makes no difference how hard you hit the organ.

"I am not terrifically impressed by the organ players around, but people like Georgie [Fame], Zoot [Money] and Brian Auger do well in the field."

Meanwhile, John McLaughlin had augmented the original trio on guitar, and had then left, at which point Heckstall-Smith joined on tenor sax. In 1964, the group became the Graham Bond Organization – with the emphasis on 'organ'. The pool of musicians on the rhythm & blues scene was by now vast, and London clubs such as The Marquee, The Flamingo and The 100 Club were packed to the rafters. John Mayall, who played the organ, guitar, and harmonica, as well as singing, was another major employer. In 1965, Eric Clapton joined Mayall's band, The Bluesbreakers, after leaving The Yardbirds, where his place was taken by Jeff Beck. Beck shared a dual-guitar line-up with Jimmy Page for a while before Page went off to form Led Zeppelin. Meanwhile, with Graham Bond on heroin, Ginger Baker had taken over the running of the Graham Bond Organization, and had sacked Jack Bruce. By now, Eric Clapton wasn't enjoying the constant touring with The Bluesbreakers, and he asked Baker to join his new band. Then Clapton brought in Bruce – despite the animosity between drummer and bassist – and in 1966 Cream was formed.

In the midst of the mayhem the three organists Bond mentioned in *Melody Maker* were managing to make a name for themselves. Georgie Fame, born Clive Powell in 1943, joined singer Billy Fury's band, The Blue Flames, in 1961. After a dispute with the singer, the band decided to stick together, and started what would turn out to be a fabled three-year stint at The Flamingo in London. The band recorded live there, and also recorded a single for Columbia. 'Yeh Yeh' was an

Brian Auger & The Trinity (top left) ; Zoot Money (top right); Georgie Fame & The Blue Flames (bottom).

earworm of a tune that reached Number One in the UK charts, a perky romp that combined the UK 'beat' with a soul sensibility. Fame was, and still is, a singer/player with his eye on the Great American Songbook, Hoagy Carmichael being a huge influence. And he's a stylist who uses Hammond (initially an M-2 spinet, which is small and has no percussion) to propel his often jazz-influenced music. In the blues spectrum he's definitely down at the jazzy end, never indulging in rock-style electric guitar blues. In the 1970s he formed a duo with organist Alan Price of The Animals, another player/singer who was happier with Hammond as a rhythm section component than as a lead instrument. The two organists had a TV show, *The Price of Fame*, that brought them a large audience.

The names on the posters at The Flamingo at this time would have included Georgie Fame & The Blue Flames, The Animals (including Alan Price), and a pianist and organist called Zoot Money. In 1961, Money had formed The Big Roll Band, an outfit destined to last to this day, which at one point included guitarist Andy Summers, later to join The Police. Stints with Korner's Blues Incorporated and Eric Burdon's New Animals ensued, giving him a music business longevity equal to Georgie Fame's. He even got together with Alan Price in the 1990s in Alan Price & The Electric Blues Company.

The third name in Graham Bond's grudging list of fellow organists is Brian Auger, another player with a long career. In the early 1960s he was carving a reputation as a jazz pianist, playing all-night sets at The Flamingo, winning awards, and including the likes of John McLaughlin in his band. Then he decided to jump aboard the rhythm & blues train. Hearing Jimmy Smith's 'Back At The Chicken Shack' coming out of speakers in a shop in Shepherd's Bush, London, in 1965, Auger acquired a Hammond C-3 (easier to get hold of than the B-3 in the UK, for some reason) and founded a band with singers Long John Baldry, formerly with Alexis Korner, Rod Stewart, and Julie Driscoll, whom he had discovered in his manager's office answering fan mail for The Yardbirds.

The group became Steampacket. Auger wasn't convinced though, and after the band had collapsed within a year he hatched a plan to "make a bridge between the separate scenes of jazz and rock. I wanted to meld R&B rhythms with jazz harmonics and solos."[9] The new outfit, Trinity, released its first album, *Open*, in 1967. The album was followed by a hit single, 'This Wheel's On Fire', a psychedelic cover version of a song from Bob Dylan's unreleased Basement Tapes. Piano and strings carry the track, and the organ is left to supply an ever-evolving upwards glissando at the end of the chorus, after "This wheel shall explode. …". Auger also gets to solo over the outro, in a chordal, bluesy, non-jazz, and slightly clumsy style.

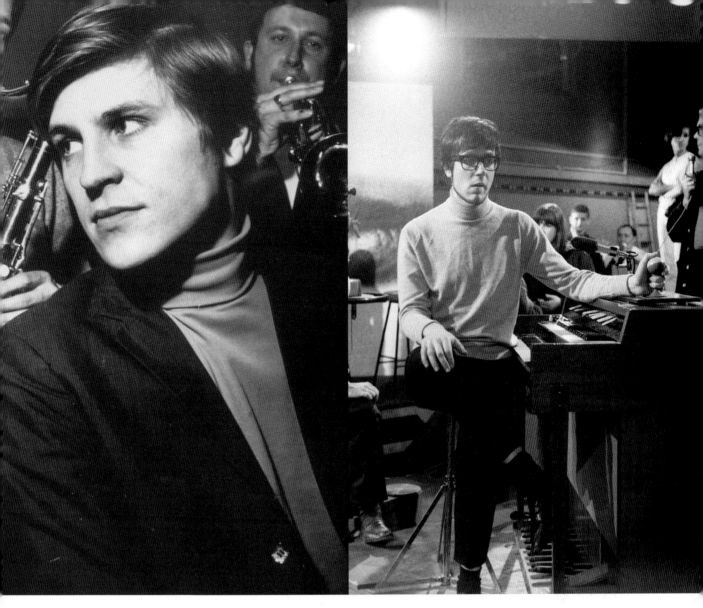

Alan Price (left); Manfred Mann (right)

Next came a 1968 album without Driscoll, *Definitely What*, which misses the mark for me. It lacks Auger's rock energy and the first track, an orchestral/Hammond contortion of The Beatles' 'A Day In The Life' is to be avoided. No, don't even be tempted out of curiosity.

In 1969, Julie Driscoll returned for the double album, *Streetnoise*, and the band returned to form. As a consequence of a lack of writing time, the album is heavy on covers, particularly from the show *Hair*, but Auger contributes some instrumental originals, and Driscoll explores areas as yet uncharted, including a folk element in 'A Word About Colour' and 'Vauxhall To Lambeth Bridge'. The rhythm section are Clive Thacker on drums and Dave Ambrose on bass, and they deserve credit for the right combination of solidity and drive.

It's the cover of Richie Havens's 'Indian Rope Man' that has resonated down the years in Hammond lore, and with good reason. Opening with repetitive organ chords, Auger adds Hohner Clavinet for that extra bite when there's no guitar in sight. (Stevie Wonder was trying the same thing.) The song is basically a D minor riff, with a few harmonic descending touches and a break for respite before kicking off again. Auger has a couple of bites at the solo cherry, which he seems to relish, but with drawbars set somewhere around 888866000 the sound is more to do with pushing amps and overdrive than the Hammond itself. It's energetic, bluesy, and all the things rock organ set out to be. To say that it doesn't have the soloistic and harmonic flair of a Larry Young or a Richard 'Groove' Holmes track is not to compare like with like. Probably none of the British rockers are as neat with their fingers as Jimmy Smith, but their playing serves the music in its energy and rawness, and there was much more to come. **Sound And Style 10, p134, CD track 26.**

WITH MANFRED MANN, ALTHOUGH HE HAD A JAZZ AND CLASSICAL EDUCATION IN SOUTH AFRICA, THE MIX IS RHYTHM & BLUES, POP, AND JAZZ, IN THAT ORDER.

Not that it's all rawness with The Trinity. Driscoll and Auger's version of the Doors classic, 'Light My Fire', starts out with some very tasteful semi-Baroque organ lines under the restrained vocal; as Driscoll picks up the intensity, Auger piles on the drawbars to raise the emotional pitch. Elsewhere on the album, Auger's instrumental armoury expands to include a clavinet-driven track, 'Ellis Island', and piano on Miles Davis's 'All Blues'. 'I've Got Life' takes a gospel-flavoured groove and cleverly works it into a 7/8 rhythm, anticipating all the tricky time signatures of progressive rock, although Auger took his cue from Dave Brubeck.

The Auger band with the longest legs has been his Oblivion Express, which he started in 1970. It's still around, nearly 40 years later, albeit without originals Jim Mullen (guitar), Barry Dean (bass), and Robbie McIntosh (who went on to drum with The Average White Band before succumbing to heroin). The 1970 debut album *Oblivion Express* finds Auger in burning mode and more comfortable stretching out. The arrangement and concept encapsulates the aims of jazz-rock, coupling investigative jazz solos with a rock rhythm section sensibility. Mullen's guitar certainly adds to the mix, and production and engineering standards are high, courtesy of Eddie Offord. A John McLaughlin track, 'Dragon Song', stands out compositionally and for Auger's solo. The third Oblivion Express album, *Second Wind* (1972), sets the style for the next few decades. Funk and soul influences join

THE PLAYERS – CLASSIC HAMMOND ORGAN

the jazz, and riff-based rock is put aside. Eddie Harris's 'Freedom Jazz Dance', which Miles Davis had recorded in 1966 with Tony Williams, makes a groovy appearance.

So does the Hammond always find its way back to jazz? Certainly with Fame and Auger the jazz quotient is fairly high. But with Manfred Mann, although he had a jazz and classical education in South Africa, the mix is rhythm & blues, pop, and jazz, in that order. When Mann came to London in 1961, he found himself in a band with the ubiquitous Graham Bond, but he became a bandleader in his own right when Paul Jones joined him in 1962 to form The Manfreds. Bob Dylan dropped by The Marquee club in 1964 and declared the band to be "real groovy". Mann returned the compliment, recording a large number of Dylan covers over the next 10 years: 'With God On Our Side', 'If You Gotta Go, Go Now', 'Just Like A Woman', and 'The Mighty Quinn'. Another C-3 player, Mann later embraced the Minimoog and went so far as to pronounce, "I'm more a piano player. Hammond players are specialists, and I'm not a good Hammond player, so I thought it was best for me to put it away."[10] Nevertheless the Manfred Mann sound, as heard on his string of 1960s hits – '5-4-3-2-1', 'Do Wah Diddy Diddy', 'Sha La La', 'Pretty Flamingo', and so on – will always be remembered as dominated by organ rather than guitar.

The British rhythm & blues scene spawned a myriad of new bands, constantly splitting, joining, and fragmenting again like demented atoms. Though the wave was as much about a new approach to guitar playing and amplification as it was about musical style, the Hammond was also central to that sound and to the London club environment where rock first met jazz.

Rocking (and rolling)

Outside of the London rhythm & blues scene, other British cities had their own musical networks. Noddy Holder of Slade has memories of the club scene: "Then this spotty kid on the organ suddenly opened his mouth and screamed 'I love the way she walks …' and launched into an old John Lee Hooker number. Gosh, my mouth fell open and I felt a chill down my spine! That was the night I discovered rhythm & blues for the first time."[11] The kid was Stevie Winwood, performing with his brother Muff on bass, Spencer Davis on guitar, and Dave Black on drums.

It's a long and winding road from 1965 to 2003, but that's the time-span of Steve Winwood's recording career. From *Sittin' And Thinkin'*, an EP released on Fontana in 1965, to the CD *About Time* is one heck of a journey, and one that I suspect is not over yet. Through all that time, Winwood has had one of the best voices in rock; strong, plaintive, but always accurate. Its emotive high end sizzles with soulful conviction. That voice that has propelled some impressive line-ups, from the early days of The Spencer Davis Group, through Traffic and Blind Faith, to the hit solo albums of the 1980s and the recent solo projects. And running alongside that voice has been the trusty Hammond.

There is no organ on that first EP, just piano, but it wasn't long in arriving. In 1966 the group released its second album, with Steve on organ on 'Georgia On My Mind', showcasing some well-chosen fills between vocal phrases. By 1967 the organ was on full throttle, powering the massive hits 'Gimme Some Lovin'' and 'I'm A Man', the latter the last hit before the brothers left to take on the world, one with star status, the other as a successful record industry executive with Chris Blackwell at Island. The organ part on 'Gimme Some Lovin'' has to be one of the most instantly recognisable Hammond riffs ever, based on what sounds to me like 888855500, the smattering of top harmonics emphasised by second-harmonic percussion. The lower manual understates the verse before Leslie and upper drawbars pile in through the bridge to the full-on chorus. Classic. **Sound And Style 11a, p134, CD track 27.**

If music business success is a matter of having the talent, then being in the right place at the right time, Steve Winwood did well by turning up at the Record Plant studios in New York City in May 1968. He wasn't alone, by all accounts. Jack Casady (who ended up on bass), guitarist Larry Coryell, and numerous others were at the court of the guitar king, Jimi Hendrix, who was recording the album that was to become *Electric Ladyland*. The track that was squeezed out of that long night, 'Voodoo Chile', features Steve on B-3 in a two-way exchange of blues-marinated phrases over a fairly stock D minor riff that leaves plenty of potential for top-octave upper-manual action. There appears to be genuine interplay going on; it's Steve who strays into major tonality after the drum break, but it's quickly pounced upon by Hendrix. The grounding Winwood received at an early age, accompanying blues masters Muddy Waters, John Lee Hooker et al on their UK tours, pays off a thousand-fold. **Sound And Style 11b, p136, CD track 28.**

With Traffic, Winwood continued to push boundaries, taking responsibility for arranging tracks and pretty much drawing up the prospectus for the next decade of musical exploration. Traffic's keen ability to absorb blues, jazz-rock, experimentation, music hall, and even folk rock might have eventually been the band's downfall.

From the late 1970s, Winwood turned his hand to a series of commercially

Steve Winwood: full of soulful conviction.

successful albums. The fourth of them, *Back In The High Life* (1986), sports some unfeasibly large 1980s drum sounds but also includes several rocking Hammond tracks. 'Freedom Overspill' interweaves B-3 with a spitting brass section, sounding almost like two manuals of the same instrument, while 'Split Decision' is a full-on down-home rocker. However, Steve Winwood grew tired of making music for the marketplace and made a dignified withdrawal from the intensity of the music business, while still producing music steeped in the history of the B-3. *About Time* (2003) is quite a loose set, combining the Latin sensibilities of guitarist Jose Neto with the earthiness of Winwood's Hammond style. 'Bully' remains funky while

showcasing a vast array of B-3 texture, and 'Horizon', with its gorgeous acoustic guitar/B-3 pad combination, harks back to earlier times. A special CD package includes bonus live tracks, as well as DVD footage that is very handy for sneaking a look at the playing style. No secrets here; while he may not technically be in the realms of the more straight-ahead jazzers, it's solid and heart-felt playing. And guess what, the final track on the bonus CD is 'Voodoo Chile'. It lacks the magic of the original, but it is interesting to hear Winwood singing the song.

Diving back into the late 1960s, the circus of rock music was in full swing. No jazz-rock or funk yet, just what was soon to become known as hard rock, with maybe a few classical and psychedelic leanings and the pervasive influence of the blues. This is the era just pre-synthesizer, and keyboard set-ups are still basically piano and organ. But for one player, at least, the Hammond was plenty to be going on with.

He was almost lost to the acting profession, but Jon Lord seemed to be attached at the hip to music. He was classically trained from an exceedingly early age, and the sounds of J.S. Bach would stay with him and become incorporated into projects right down the line. He also listened to the jazz explosion Hammond players, Smith, McGriff, and McDuff, and with them came the influence of the blues. Lord said of his work in the late 1960s: "That was one of the most fascinating parts of my life, trying to make the Hammond organ sound like a rock instrument rather than sound like a jazz and blues instrument … and I think I did in the end, I got there."[12]

Lord worked that problem out with Deep Purple, the band he formed in 1967/8. He and guitarist Ritchie Blackmore shaped the band's organ/guitar front line, while bassist Nick Simper and drummer Ian Paice formed the rhythm section. Singer Rod Evans completed the line-up of this first version of the band. *The Book of Taliesyn* (1969), Deep Purple's second album, includes the track 'Wring That Neck' (known as 'Hard Road' in the US), recorded live. It includes a solo Hammond intro that reveals the whole classical side of Lord's playing: diminished chords, chromatic and harmonic minor scale runs, large chords with vibrato, sus4 chords resolving in a plagal way. Then he sets up the rhythm for the track, sharing lead line harmony with Blackmore in a fast shuffle with an intricate eighth-note melody. **Sound And Style 12, p138, CD track 29.**

All the elements were in place for what sounds to me more like a confrontation between classical and blues than a fusion. The subsequent album went further down that road – too far for some. *Concerto For Group And Orchestra*, featuring the

Jon Lord of Deep Purple: making the Hammond sound like a rock instrument.

Royal Phiharmonic Orchestra with composer Malcolm Arnold at the helm, is a strange beast. It combines Deep Purple's rock'n'roll with Russian-influenced orchestral interludes, but it's the change of personnel that marks it out. Roger Glover comes in on bass, and Ian Gillan on vocals. The stage is set, as they say, for the classic Deep Purple hard rock albums, *Deep Purple In Rock* (1970), which featured 'Child In Time', and *Machine Head* (1972), which introduced 'Smoke On The Water'. By this time, not only was Gillan in remarkable voice, the two instrumental front-liners were also fired up. A case in point was 'Highway Star', from *Machine Head*, a tough old rocker of a track where the organ is nestled alongside the guitar, breaking out for a heavily treated fuzz solo, those harmonic minor lines lending an air of Eastern mystery over descending minor chords.

At some point around the change of line-up, Lord abandoned the Leslie setup and started playing through Marshall amps, via various boxes, so that he could compete on a volume level. One of his boxes was a ring modulator, an effect that delivers 'clangy', bell-like sounds. The effects gave the Hammond an extra bite, maybe even distorting its origins to render it almost unrecognisable, but integrating it into a Heavy Metal band sound and thereby enhancing its longevity.

The British rock scene of the late 1960s and 1970s was choc-a-bloc with bands taking detours into heavy rock. Uriah Heap's *Very 'Eavy, Very 'Umble* finds Ken Hensley strutting his stuff on Hammond and other keyboards, including Mellotron. Vincent Crane is another case in point; the band Atomic Rooster was largely his vehicle, kicking off in 1969 with Carl Palmer in the drumseat. They had both worked with The Crazy World of Arthur Brown in preceding years, Crane co-writing the band's very popular 'Fire', which still sounds like a good pop record and has Hammond absolutely at the top of the mix; in fact the organ sounds closer than the reverbed vocals. The chorus 'Fire!' has a handy Hammond answering riff, which the brass take up later, and Crane uses Brian Auger's smudge technique to build the sustained chromatic rising chords of 'You're gonna burn', to accentuate the drama.

It's hard to find anything quite as entertaining in the Atomic Rooster catalogue, but that was probably not their aim. 'Breakthrough', from 1971's *In Hearing Of Atomic Rooster* includes some high-energy blues riffs, with Crane obviously having a ball with the drummer, Rick Parnell. A highlight is the breakdown-followed-by-buildup that exploits all the second-harmonic and drawbar possibilities at hand. Again, there's no Leslie, but guitar amps aplenty.

At the time of writing Led Zeppelin have just played a reunion gig in London,

Procol Harum (top), featuring Matthew Fisher on Hammond; Pink Floyd (below), featuring Rick Wright.

to much acclaim (and much ringing in the ears). John Paul Jones, primarily the bassist with the band, is a dark horse. Having learned in church, then worked as a session musician/arranger (often with Jimmy Page), he was well equipped to handle Hammond/keyboard parts, broadening the band's sound palette. Hammonds were used on stage and in the studio. Zeppelin's solution to the live Leslie volume problem was to stick the cabinet in a dressing room offstage and mike it up. In the studio Jones used initially an M-100 then a C-3. On 'Thank You', from *Led Zeppelin II* (1969), Jones plays it churchy and pure, adding vibrato for the bridge. 'Since I've Been Loving You', from Led Zeppelin III (1970), is a Leslied-up track that would be a regular on stage. 'Night Flight', from 1975's *Physical Graffiti*, has a pad of swirly Hammond, with little upper harmonic action. And 'Kashmir', from the same album, has a touch of organ, or it could be Mellotron.

Away from hard and heavy rock, other bands were taking shape, with their own takes on the rock, pop, jazz, psychedelic blend. A chief contender for most interesting rock band of the late 1960s would have to be Pink Floyd. Under Syd Barrett's zany but inspired influence, Pink Floyd's set list was originally led by pop songs, which gave them successful singles such as 'Arnold Layne' and 'See Emily Play', both from 1967. Using a Farfisa organ early on, keyboard player Rick Wright included a Hammond M-100 for the first album, *The Piper At The Gates Of Dawn* (1967). More often than not the Hammond is textural, and the sound treatments disguise the source, but I think one of the passages on 'Matilda Mother' is Hammond. If not, it's definitely an organ, and it plays an Asian–tinged melody that's extremely evocative. The same texture takes the track out. This album is full of extraordinary moments. Take the beginning of 'Flaming', a low cluster of organ notes, then straight into the song. Over the years Wright was to use a C-3, an M-102 and an RT-3, mostly through a Leslie 122 cabinet. The RT-3 is an interesting model that included an expanded 32-note pedalboard and added pedal sounds of a reed and a string timbre. Aside from that it was identical to a C-3.

The M-100 crops up again in the story of Matthew Fisher, keyboard player with the band Procol Harum, who famously went to court to prove that he wrote the organ intro melody to 'A Whiter Shade Of Pale' (1967). When the record is the most played record in the UK over the last 70 years, and has been covered by just about everyone possessing half a larynx, this is quite a big deal. A ruling in the appeal courts in 2008 said that Fisher should get a songwriting credit but no royalties because of the length of time he waited before staking his claim.But what does it sound like? For the intro line we're in church, 688800000 or close, and the Leslie spins for the line "And so it was…".**Sound And Style 13, p138, CD track 30.**

The Grateful Dead in 1983, featuring Brent Mydland.

Meanwhile, there was a parallel psychedelic universe happening in the USA with The Byrds, The Grateful Dead, and later Jefferson Airplane spearheading the movement from the West Coast. Guitarist Jerry Garcia's Grateful Dead defy categorisation. A blend of blues, rock, folk, and exploratory jazz begins to describe it; sometimes it's directionless and shambolic, sometimes it's focused. Sometimes founder Ron 'Pigpen' McKernan plays Hammond (or other organs), and sometimes, after 1968, it's Tom Constanten. Studio albums struggled to capture their essence, but live, their sprawling solos had the space to breathe expansively. They are perhaps best represented on *Live Dead* (1969), where there reside three tracks of around 10-15 minutes and 'Dark Star', a mind-expanding chemically-altered 23:18. The Hammond gets a best supporting role nomination overall, but a starring part in 'Death Don't Have No Mercy' (written by bluesman Rev. Gary Davis), where Constanten weaves lines sparely, seamlessly, and naturally through

FOLLOWING PAGE **Greg Allman with The Allman Brothers.**

the fabric of the song. The sound is similar to Steve Winwood's on *Electric Ladyland,* lightening and darkening responsively when required. The organ finds a useful place in the abstract 'Feedback', and is the mainstay of 'Saint Stephen'. After Constanten left, in 1970, the organ stool reverted to Pigpen, then passed to Brent Mydland for the next 11 years.

Where the Dead led, The Allman Brothers were on their heels, with an equal interest in extended rock improvisation. When stretching out, Duane and Greg Allman's band were in general more urgent than The Dead. To compare like with like, *At Fillmore East* (1971) contains edited live versions of songs such as 'Statesboro Blues' and 'Stormy Monday'. The former displays Greg's solid organ rhythm playing, and the latter his textural blues colours; he also contributes a double-time solo over the sequence. Also recorded at Fillmore East, but released on 1972's *Eat A Peach*, is the lengthy but worthwhile 'Mountain Jam', which finds the band improvising without any air of self-indulgence: the arrangements are moulded and honed, and any roughness in the playing sandpapered down.

The same could not be said of rockers Vanilla Fudge, who, a few years earlier, had been strutting versions of Beatles tunes, Motown singles, and anything else they could slow down and psychedelically rockify. The big hit was the Supremes' 'You Keep Me Hanging On' (1967), with Mark Stein's opening Hammond mood blasted to the outer regions of Mars by the equally enthusiastic drumming of Carmine Appice.

Aside from the excesses of rock'n'roll, the figure who dominates 1960s rock, Bob Dylan, had hardened and electrified his sound as the decade progressed. Al Kooper was in for the ride on keyboards, including Hammond, after his performance on 'Like A Rolling Stone' (1965). He originally turned up hoping to play guitar, but inveigled himself into the session by coming up with the famous organ part for the song, despite not being an organ player. He would continue to play with Dylan until the fateful motor bike accident in 1966 that took Dylan out of the loop for a few years and linked him up with the musicians who would come to be known as the 'The Band'.

Progressing, fusing, and generally funking

In the 1970s, the synthesizer began to play a prominent role in keyboard music-making. But the Hammond continued to thrive, especially in the music of two giants of progressive rock. Both Keith Emerson and Rick Wakeman expanded their arsenals of keyboards over the decade, but not initially at the expense of the organ; the trusty servant continued to be used alongside the new breed of synthesizer. Other rock keyboardists also kept plying their Hammond trade, including Tony Banks, Rod Argent, and, as we have seen, Brian Auger.

Keith Emerson was born in 1944. His dad played accordion, and Keith picked out tunes on the piano before launching himself into both classical music and jazz with, it seems, equal enthusiasm. Hearing Jack McDuff left an indelible impression, and before long the piano player found himself seated one day at the L-100 organ, playing with a band called The Nice. That came about because Emerson, Lee Jackson (bass and vocals), and David O'List (guitar) had been the backing band for the American soul singer P.P. Arnold. When the band caught the attention of a record company, Brian Davison completed the line-up on drums. The Nice's material was made up of pop/psychedelic vocal originals and tunes such as 'America', taken from the Leonard Bernstein show *West Side Story*, and 'Rondo', based on Dave Brubeck's 'Blue Rondo A La Turk'. The playing was strong, and the arrangements intricate but musically handled.

On their 1971 album *Elegy*, released after the band's demise, The Nice tackled the third movement of Tchaikovsky's 'Pathétique' Symphony. In terms of tight playing, and wringing all you can from an L-100, it's stunning, and Emerson's technique is as solid as you'll ever find. In their short career, The Nice had done more than anyone else to openly combine the classics and modern rock/jazz. The record *Five Bridges* (1970) pitted The Nice against The Sinfonia Of London and incorporated music by Sibelius, Bach, and Guida, committing the band to classical crossover more than Jon Lord's venture with Deep Purple had managed.

AL KOOPER TURNED UP HOPING TO PLAY GUITAR, BUT INVIEGLED HIMSELF INTO THE SESSION ON ORGAN BY COMING UP WITH THE FAMOUS PART FOR THE SONG.

The Nice had to give way, however, to one of the supergroups of the 1970s, Emerson Lake & Palmer. Bassist Greg Lake came from the disintegrating King Crimson, while Carl Palmer had been with Arthur Brown and Atomic Rooster. The interesting thing when comparing The Nice with ELP is the rhythm track; despite the superstar status of the later band, the rhythm section sounds looser and more forced. But what ELP does have is power, as the audience at the 1970 Isle of Wight festival found out. This was not a moment for shyness, it was about extreme showbiz and extravagant flamboyance.

For Emerson that meant sticking his collection of Hitler Youth daggers between the keys of the L-100 to sustain notes, then tipping it around the stage, and so on.

Emerson Lake & Palmer (1970) includes adaptations of Bartók and Janácek, the latter in the appropriately named 'Knife-Edge'. Dark and dramatic Hammond chords launch the bass guitar riff, then Lake sings of things visionary before the Hammond is given space to cut loose. Whilst Emerson owns up to a preference for 888800000 with fast third-harmonic percussion and C3 vibrato, this sounds more like 888000800, the 1 3/5' drawbar providing an element of 'al dente'. The sound is raw too, worlds away from gospel lush and closer to Jimmy McGriff's sound, which was intentional on Emerson's part. 'Hoedown' from 1972's *Trilogy* is an arrangement of a tune from Aaron Copland's *Rodeo*. It employs classic 888000000 Hammond settings in an exuberant D to C jam. Emerson isn't afraid to delve into the cracks between these tonalites, passing in and out of consonance along the way.

Elsewhere Emerson's organ can sound full-on and churchy, as in the live Mussorgsky adaptation, *Pictures At An Exhibition*; or it is radically altered by recording technique, using just percussion and pushing it up in the mix. Which brings us to 'Tarkus', from the 1971 album of the same name. Here percussion rules in the complex doubling of lines in the longest and most compositionally advanced piece of 'prog rock' to date. 'Stones Of Years', the second section, sports a swaggering Hammond solo, with the percussion emphasised by loudness of keyclick. **Sound And Style 14, p140, CD track 31.**

If Rudy Van Gelder was the man to record the soul-jazz B-3, Eddie Offord was the man for the British prog rock C-3. He must almost have gone straight from producing and engineering ELP's *Tarkus* to Yes's 1972 album, *Close To The Edge*. Yes had formed in 1968 and by this time included Rick Wakeman, who had taken over from Tony Kaye on keyboards in 1971, joining Steve Howe on guitar, and the two founders, vocalist Jon Anderson and bassist Chris Squire. Wakeman used a battery of keyboards: a Steinway piano, a Mellotron 400, several Minimoogs, an RMI electric piano/harpsichord, and of course a C-3. I would guess that Wakeman had a less intuitive feel for the Hammond than Emerson, but it's hard to resist at those points in an arrangement that call for sheer sustained power. Piano is too jangly; the Mellotron's textures are too soft; and synthesizers were not yet polyphonic. Which just leaves the Hammond. Apparently Wakeman didn't like the design of the B-3, preferring the C-3.

Keith Emerson with The Nice (top); The Strawbs featuring Rick Wakeman (below).

There aren't too many places to listen to Wakeman's Hammond work with Yes; he joined for the album *Fragile* (1971), and left after *Tales From Topographic Oceans* (1973), which is more of a synth album. 1972's *Close To The Edge*, however, reveals a reliance on the Hammond from 'Siberian Khatru' to the title track. The 1973 live album, *Yessongs*, also features Hammond on several other tracks, 'Perpetual Change' being the best example. Wakeman uses it for heavy punctuation and triumphal sequences, seldom for quiet passages. The language of the music itself is like no other, formed mostly by the trio of Anderson, Squire and Howe, with Wakeman cast as an onlooker. The compositions include sections in complex time signatures along with anthemic yet mystical refrains; the whole is impressive, and refreshingly shows no reliance on existing classical themes.

The organ style, as revealed on 'Close To The Edge', the title track of the album, consists of tracking the guitar melody with harmonic percussion engaged, supporting the chorale guitar theme when it arrives, and finally having a couple of bars to itself before the vocals come in. In those couple of bars, Wakeman is stepping up through an F major broken chord pattern, with a sound something like 888000346 with percussion. The organ solo relies too much on one sort of diatonic lick to hold interest for these ears, lacking the harmonic interest of a Larry Young or even the 'between the keys' of Emerson. I'm not sure that Wakeman was ever comfortable with Yes. When it comes to his own compositions, the language is straighter and more classical, lacking the

BY THE MID 1970S, HAMMOND ORGANS WERE STARTING TO LOOK PREHISTORIC, DESPITE THE LAUNCH OF NEW MODELS.

incisiveness of a Yes track, but that's just my humble opinion. What Wakeman did very effectively was to combine a cornucopia of keyboard resources resourcefully into a band arrangement, and in his execution of that combination he was charismatic and musical.

The UK rock scene had one other influential figure in its midst, the organist Rod Argent. He had been through the 1960s with rock/pop band the Zombies, featuring the velvet tones of Colin Blunstone, for whom he'd written several hits, including 'She's Not There' and 'Tell Her No'. In 1968, he formed his own band, Argent. Their breakthrough came with 1972's 'Hold Your Head Up', a hit single that is still iconic in its use of the Hammond. It's from the band's third and probably strongest album, *All Together Now*, which was produced by Chris White, who had been the Zombies' bass player. He co-wrote the tune with Argent, and to describe it as a

THE PLAYERS – CLASSIC HAMMOND ORGAN

stomper is probably an understatement. The riff and groove are dead simple; it's what goes on top that makes it sparkle.

Right from the off, glistening tonewheels trill away in the upper harmonic region before the guitar riff kicks in, with the Hammond jauntily filling the gaps. Come the chorus however, the organ reinforces the chorus line with a swoop up to D and down again. Another verse/chorus follows, then the solo. From the start you know this one's going to take time; no flash frills but genuine exploration. The sound is set around 888050220 with second-harmonic percussion, but heftily overdriven. Argent makes full use of the D pedal, setting up other chords over it in contrapuntal fashion. It is interesting, too, that he uses a C-sharp in the first few bars, in the same way that Miles Davis does when constructing an otherwise conventional D Dorian solo on 'So What'. **Sound And Style 15, p142, CD track 32.**

With Brian Auger and Rod Argent on board, the Hammond rock scene in the UK was sailing steadily with a following breeze, but a serious weather warning had been received, and the advent of synths, and eventually (and more usefully) polyphonic synths, heralded rough seas ahead for Hammond. In the mid 1970s, Hammond organs were starting to look prehistoric, despite the company launching some new models in the mid 1960s. The X-66 and X-77 had updated styling and features, but at around $10,000 they probably weren't jumping off the shelves. The tonewheel arrangement was compromised by installing only 12 high pitches, which were then electronically divided to complete the whole range. Laurens Hammond had bowed out of the company in 1960, retiring to Connecticut. The last batch of B-3s was produced in 1975, and you would be forgiven for thinking that was it, end of story; but the tonewheel organ had legs yet.

In the USA, the situation was similar to the UK, in that players were moving out of the specialist organ field and incorporating Hammond into a wider collection of keyboards. One such was Bill Payne, a pianist and organist whose life-changing moment must have been when Lowell George asked him to join Little Feat. George had been gigging with Frank Zappa's Mothers of Invention, and Frank had suggested to him, in the nicest possible way, that he form his own band. Recruited along with Payne were Richie Hayward (drums) and Roy Estrada (bass). With George on guitar and vocals, that's the way things stood. In 1972, after two albums, Estrada left, perhaps thinking the band was going nowhere. He was replaced by Kenny Gradney, and the band was augmented by Paul Barrere on guitar and percussionist Sam Clayton.

With George increasingly entangled with drugs, Barrere and Payne took more of a front seat with the songwriting, leading to three excellent albums, *Feats Don't*

Fail Me Now (1974), *The Last Record Album* (1975) and *Time Loves A Hero* (1977). Payne's characteristic contribution is electric piano and piano, but the organ is featured on tracks such as 'Hi Roller', from *Time Loves A Hero*. Stylistically right in the pocket, Payne has to elbow his way through a crowd of horns, but it's worth it; the Hammond shines. Payne has since been involved in *2B3: The Toronto Sessions*, an album of organ duets that has become a talking point of the Hammond world. Aside from Payne, it features, among others, Lance Anderson, Richard Bell of The Band, and Richie Hayward, Payne's partner in Little Feat.

Mention of Bell, who joined The Band in the 1990s, takes me to the curious case of Garth Hudson, whom I had pictured at a Hammond during his time with The Band and Bob Dylan. In fact the instrument he plays is a Lowrey organ, apparently as a result of a very conscious decision. It suffices to say that his playing with The Band, on what was probably a more orchestral instrument, was exemplary. Hudson was also responsible for recording Dylan's famous 'basement tapes'.

Al Kooper has had a hell of a music career. He played with Bob Dylan; he discovered Lynyrd Skynyrd in 1972 and produced their first album; he formed The Blues Project; he played sessions with just about everybody, The Rolling Stones included; he joined the faculty at Berklee College Of Music in Boston, Massachusetts; and not least, he has been sampled by anyone who's anyone in the hip-hop scene, notably The Beastie Boys (who have also sampled Richard 'Groove' Holmes).

Many might think that just putting together Blood, Sweat & Tears was enough of a contribution. Gigging at the Café Au Go Go in Greenwich Village, New York City, Kooper injured himself, and the sight of the blood on his organ keys is said to have inspired the name. Kooper formed the band in 1967 after The Blues Project fell apart. He brought in Jim Fielder on bass, Steve Katz on guitar, drummer Bobby Colomby, and a brass section made up of Randy Brecker and Jerry Weiss (trumpets), Dick Halligan (trombone), and Fred Lipsius (alto saxophone). Audiences had heard nothing like it: complex brass arrangements with blues underpinnings and jazz soloing.

The first album, *Child Is Father To The Man*, came in 1968. 'House In The Country' reveals Kooper to have had an ear for harmony way ahead of his time, allied to an almost British sense of pop. The organ chugs along, happy in its rhythm section role. 'Somethin' Goin' On' features a Hammond sound with a top-end harmonic presence, slicing through the brass. Kooper left after the first album. Later versions of B, S & T, starting with the second album, *Blood, Sweat & Tears*,

The Zombies (top); Little Feat (below).

diluted the jazz, but not the organ usage: it features particularly on 'You've Made Me So Very Happy', with its full-on gospel Leslie, and 'God Bless The Child', with its Hammond pad.

Carlos Santana's bands have included some fine musicians, including a brace of keyboard players by the names of Gregg Rolie and Tom Coster. Rolie was in at the beginning, having joined up with the guitarist in the original Santana Blues Band in 1966. After several changes of personnel in the percussion department, Santana recorded their first album, *Santana*, but before it was even released secured a gig at the Woodstock Music And Art Festival of 1969. The festival was filmed for perhaps the most celebrated of all concert movies. Its release in 1970 immortalised Rolie's Hammond solo on 'Soul Sacrifice'. The band is certainly fired up by the intensity of the occasion, as is Rolie, easing his way into the solo and picking out notes to add Leslie to. The effect of that is to cleverly expressive, adding emotion to some notes in a phrase. The solo stays rooted in A minor but having gone through a choppy section, exploits every last drop from held top Cs. **Sound And Style 16, p144, CD track 33.**

Another ploy of Rolie's is to control the brightness of the upper manual by switching percussion on and off, thereby disabling the 1' drawbar. His solo on the studio version of 'Evil Ways', from *Santana*, employs this technique. Rolie sat at the organ from 1966 to 1972 and from 1983 to 1984. Tom Coster took the chair from 1972 to 1978. During this time he contributed to six Santana albums, from *Caravanserai* (1972) to *Moonflower* (1977). Coster has described his amp setup: "To compete with Carlos, I used to run my organ through two Leslies and direct into Twin Reverb amplifiers. The key was for the house mixer to amalgamate those sounds, so that one wasn't more present than the other and it wouldn't sound like a Farfisa as opposed to the beautiful sound of the Hammond."[13] Coster favours 888800000 with fingers poised to access higher drawbars when necessary.

Santana's unique recipe was to blend Latin and rock. Elsewhere another musical mixer, Bob Marley, was employing the services of a Hammond in the context of reggae music. Bernard 'Touter' Harvey and two London session men, John 'Rabbit' Bundrick and Jean Alain Roussel, claim to have put down various keyboard instruments on Marley tracks, and it's not easy to sort out who did what, when, and where. Roussel insists he arranged and played Hammond on 'No Woman No Cry', 'Natty Dread', and 'Lively Up Yourself' from 1974's *Natty Dread*, and had a similar involvement with 1976's *Rastaman Vibration*. Bundrick, who recorded with the likes of The Who, is credited on 1973's *Catch A Fire*, and Harvey is listed as organist and pianist also on *Natty Dread* and 1975's *Live!* album.

Carlos Santana has used many keyboard players throughout his career. This 1972 show with Buddy Miles featured Bob Hogins on Hammond.

If you compare the versions of 'No Woman, No Cry', from studio to live album, one is skippy, the other more laid-back. The Hammond in the studio is purity personified, the one on stage gospel-tinged. What is consistent in the style is the 'skank'; it's an offbeat rhythm with the right hand, offset by the left hand an eighth-note either side, and it can be swung or straight. 'Lively Up Yourself' has a fine example of the swung variety, as well as a very subtle chorused melodic doubling. 'I Shot The Sheriff', from *Live!*, has glorious Hammond, probably courtesy of Bernard 'Touter' Harvey. Sporting a sound resembling full on, the organ states the opening melody before retiring to the rhythm section for the verse. The verse skank is particularly prickly, with upper drawbar scintillation in the region of 708006366, no percussion required. **Sound And Style 17, p144, CD track 34.**

In studios across the world, Hammonds were still being oiled to keep those wheels turning. But if you'd suggested to any of the synth bands of the 1980s that some Hammond would be good on a track, your name and address would have been in the waste paper basket as you left. No, this was the era of the digital synthesizer. Yamaha's DX synths were ubiquitous, and the analogue crowd were even putting their synths under the control of MIDI, the new protocol for communication between electronic instruments. But after a brief hiatus, some musicians realised that the Hammond was what they were born to play. The way they demonstrated that was to jump aboard the club express, headed for the dance floor.

Acid jazz

Acid House music was a phenomenon of the mid 1980s, a style of pure dance music that formed the soundtrack for the rave scene. Based around the Roland TB303 bass synth and TR808 drum machine, the music was electronic, repetitive, and perfect for mass consumption. It spilled out of clubs into disused warehouses and the tranquil UK countryside. In the late 1980s, various bands took that hard dance rhythm and mixed it with the essence of the Blue Note era jazz of the 1960s and the jazz-fusion of the 1970s; the result came to be called 'acid jazz'. The DJ Gilles Peterson stumbled on the name and it inspired him to establish a record label called exactly that. Bands such as The Brand New Heavies, Incognito, and Snowboy quickly joined the Acid Jazz label. Close behind them were The James Taylor Quartet, with their albums *Mission Impossible* and *The Money Spyder*.

James Taylor of The James Taylor Quartet.

John Medeski with Medeski Martin & Wood. Chris Wood is on bass.

The organist James Taylor hails from Kent, England, and started gigging in the dark years of the Hammond: "You really didn't hear the instrument, anywhere. I was laughed at all the time for turning up with this, and they'd say, 'You could have got a DX7, mate.'"[14] There were of course organ patches on the Yamaha DX7 synthesizer, but none you'd want to hear right now. It was the musicality of the Hammond that struck Taylor, and pretty soon he had formed a band, with his brother Dave Taylor on guitar, Allan Crockford on bass, and Simon Howard on drums. They quickly established a sizeable live following, and the first recording was 'Blow-Up', a cover of Herbie Hancock's theme for the 1966 film, directed by Michelangelo Antonioni.

Films and TV of the 1960s were a frequent inspiration for Taylor, providing a slightly quaint period touch that was beefed up by the right soul-jazz elements. *Mission Impossible* (1986) itself is too early to belong to any acid-jazz school, though. Instead, nostalgia seems to be order of the day, from the quality of the reverb down to track content and delivery. He even gives us a version of Jimmy Smith's 'The Cat', sounding brighter than Smith with an 888000556 registration. Meanwhile, 'Goldfinger' and 'Mrs Robinson' serve to acquaint a new generation with the delights of the 1960s.

FILMS AND TV OF THE 1960S WERE A FREQUENT INSPIRATION FOR JAMES TAYLOR, PROVIDING A PERIOD TOUCH THAT WAS BEEFED UP BY THE SOUL-JAZZ ELEMENTS.

Further down the line, with *Get Organized* (1989), the band are tighter, and brass and vocals push the sound in more of an acid-jazz direction, even sounding like Jamiroquai on occasion. With the arrival of the 1990s the sound is a fully paid-up member of the scene. The band has an updated rhythm section on *Do Your Own Thing*, and the production is slicker, and tamer, but the material is adventurous for all that; 'Valhalla' has a harmonically unsettled bipolarity, 'Ted's Asleep' toys with a 7/8 groove, but it's the 'JTQ Theme' that displays all the hallmarks of the band and Taylor himself. With a Blood, Sweat & Tears brass fanfare for an intro, the scene is set for Blaxploitation-style wah-wah guitar and a funk bassline. Taylor's solo, given the snappy length of the track, cuts to the chase (888000000, third-harmonic percussion, and soft, fast decay). **Sound And Style 18, p146, CD track 35.**

You could say that James Taylor brought back the Hammond into 1990s consciousness; but he didn't necessarily stretch the direction of the music. John Medeski, on the other hand, has forged a contemporary-sounding trio who look

CLASSIC HAMMOND ORGAN – **THE PLAYERS**

backwards to the first jazz wave, and to The Meters, and yet have stayed right alongside modern grooves and sound influences. The trio, completed by drummer/ percussionist Billy Martin and bassist Chris Wood, simply have no fear. One minute they are in the midst of a collective abstract improvisation, the next in a hip-hop groove, playing accessible music for an audience that goes beyond just jazz fans.

Medeski, who was born in 1965, grew up in Fort Lauderdale, Florida. He learned classical piano as a child, and discovered jazz in his early teens; not just any jazz, either, but the music of avant-garde improviser Cecil Taylor, some of the densest, most thrilling, most roller-coastering keyboard playing you're likely to hear. In 1981, Medeski was playing in a club with bass genius Jaco Pastorius, who invited him to play on a country session, which he did. He was then asked to go on tour with Jaco to Japan, but apparently his mother wouldn't let him go. Medeski went on to study with George Russell and Dave Holland at the New England Conservatory in Boston, meanwhile playing with drummer Bob Moses. That connection led him to New York City, and before long Medeski found

ONE MINUTE MEDESKI MARTIN & WOOD ARE IN THE MIDST OF A COLLECTIVE ABSTRACT IMPROVISATION, THE NEXT THEY ARE IN A HIP-HOP GROOVE.

himself at the forefront of the John Zorn/Lounge Lizards/Knitting Factory scene, in the new-found company of Woods and Martin. Medeski Martin & Wood's first album, *Notes From The Underground* (1991), is the result of distilled NYC experience, exploring the possibilities of the piano trio in and outside of a groove context.

Then the Hammond struck, originally – a familiar story – as a way of getting a reliable keyboard. Medeski's Hammond of choice these days is an A-100, which is a B or C with internal speakers, but Medeski prefers it because he says it has a thicker "nastier" bottom end. On top of the organ sits a clavinet, and within reach are acoustic piano, Wurlitzer electric piano, and occasionally Mellotron. Medeski has worked at the drawbar finishing school: "I've just tried to get it so it's intuitive what all those different harmonics do … because each harmonic is a different tone and what you're doing is varying the volume of that tone by pulling the drawbars in and out, and so if you're playing a chord, suddenly that one drawbar is adding all those upper extensions and stuff…. I guess I do it to try to make it vocal; its a way that it can be expressive for me by changing it, like within a melody the way a singer would or a horn player might change the colour of the notes in the melody. That's kind of what I'm doing with the organ – trying to do."[15]

Through the 1990s, the band probed and shoved and found their just reward when Blue Note offered to record it. With the addition of DJ Logic on turntables, the band sounds fully formed on 'Combustication' (1998), a collection of groovy tunes that appeals to heart and head equally. I can see how some, leaning towards the purist end of the spectrum, might be irritated by the samples and scratching, but it seems only natural to me. In amongst it all is Medeski's highly restrained Hammond, never pushing the already lazy shuffling groove, with a great sense of economy and build. There's already tension in the feel of the swung eighth-notes (quavers); sometimes they're almost straight, others times swung like Booker T. Jones. Post-modern is probably the word: aware of the choices modernity has made available.

The Hammond is used in many ways, for textures and for lead line, but actually not so much for chordal rhythm, which tends to come from clavinet or Wurlitzer. 'Hey-Hee-Hi-Ho' eases its way in with held chorused high notes, that then melt into a melody line sounding maybe 86800000, second percussion, normal and fast. When a change of chord comes, the top line harks back to The Meters' 'Cissy Strut'. 'Latin Shuffle' changes horse midstream, metamorphosing from a piano-based Cuban pattern to an organ-based echo of Peggy Lee's 'Fever'. But there's no development of the musical idea, it's all in the sound; drawbars are being shunted about like railway carriages in a siding. **Sound And Style 19, p146, CD track 36.**

Guitarist John Scofield recorded 'Cissy Strut' on his 1989 CD *Flat Out*. On his 1998 Verve CD *A Go Go* he was joined by Medeski, Martin, and Wood. If you're looking for a straighter approach from Medeski then look no further than this album. You wouldn't say he was a 1960s organist in a blindfold test, but the instrumentation and tunes are more conventional, plus the organ is well recorded and compressed to sound close. Medeski abandons his usual restraint on 'Chank', as fingers fly in sometimes unexpected directions. These four musicians met up again, as Medeski Scofield Martin & Wood to record *Out Louder*. This time the musical input is shared, and it pays off; the guitar is more settled in the band sound, allowing for more pushing and pulling, in a railway siding kind of way.

For club jazz of the 1980s and 1990s, the updating of the groove was of prime importance, and the melodic content was self-consciously contained to draw a line between players of the 1960s and those of the 1990s. Bands like The Brand New Heavies also used Hammond in sound, if not in reality. 'Put The Funk Back In It', from *The Brand New Heavies* (1990), pumps along like a set of church organ bellows. Another approach to dealing with Hammond history was developing however, one which involved taking the language as it was, and making it speak for modern jazz ears.

Barbara Dennerlein: a composer as well as an awe-inspiring player.

The second jazz boom

There are three important figures in the jazz organ revival of the 1990s. In no particular order, they are Joey DeFrancesco, Larry Goldings and Barbara Dennerlein.

Of course, there are many other organists who have kept the torch alight, often working in clubs in a trio setting, treading the pedals with unflagging enthusiasm: one example is the UK's Mike Carr, who has built a solid career as a jazz organist since the mid 1960s, in trios with Ronnie Scott, John McLaughlin, and Jim Mullen, as well as Americans Kenny Clarke, Eddie 'Lockjaw' Davis, and Coleman Hawkins. To see him at full tilt, managing feet, comping, and soloing, is an awe-inspiring sight.

So, too, is the sight of Barbara Dennerlein at full throttle. It may be her we have to thank for the worldwide revival of interest in the Hammond. I remember being told I couldn't play the organ until I was 14 or so, as my legs wouldn't be long enough; but Barbara Dennerlein managed to kickstart a B-3 at the age of 12, with a teacher who emphasised the importance of pedals, while playing the standard jazz repertoire: "I started with organ. This is very important because I immediately learned to play the bass lines with my feet. This is the speciality of my organ playing, using hands and feet independently."[16]

Born in 1964, Barbara was performing in clubs in her home town of Munich, Germany, by the age of 15. She met and played with Jimmy Smith, met Wild Bill Davis, won organ competitions, and generally indulged her specific enthusiasm for the B-3. She was a composer right from the start, and although she had one ear on the jazz organ tradition it seems as if the other was open to other possibilities of the instrument. Thus she is rarely compared to the Smith model, partly because of her feet and partly because she doesn't want to be constrained by a preset sound vocabulary. By the mid 1980s, MIDI (Musical Instrument Digital Interface) had arrived, and it became possible to link the B-3 to other sound sources, thereby combining the Hammond sound with sampler and synthesizer sounds. For the pedals, she uses a sampled contrabass sound. The result is to show off her excellent pedal skills, as well as expanding the palette of available timbres.

The record that broke her to a larger public was *Straight Ahead*, released in 1988 on the Enja label. Her playing sounds fully formed, with a natural swing, and her writing is intriguing too, taking on board some of the harmonic and melodic zeitgeist. To illustrate, the parallel fourths with guitar on 'Bad And Blue', a mid-tempo swinger, bring to mind Mike Stern's melody style, constantly turning around on itself like a python round a trunk. Mitch Watkins is on guitar, Ronnie Burrage is on drums, and the irrepressible Ray Anderson joins later in the album on trombone. Barbara's solo on 'Bad And Blue' reveals a similar trick to that used by Richard 'Groove' Holmes, ie, perversely turning the Leslie off when the musical temperature is getting hotter.

The CDs that broke her to an international public were recorded for Verve in the 1990s, culminating in *Outhipped* in 1999. Harnessing the cream of NYC talent – Jeff 'Tain' Watts on drums, Don Alias on percussion, and a horn line-up including Steve Slagle and Darren Barrett – the swing is harder still and Dennerlein sounds as if she's having a ball, compositionally as well as in her playing. Another Holmes trademark, the whistling 1', appears on 'Jammin' and elsewhere there is much evidence of funk having taken place. 'Satisfaction' is given a smart coat of Meters-style paint, 'Outhipped' is a funky 7/4, heavy on the percussion, and 'In The Mud' sounds almost like The Brecker Brothers with funk guitar and a quartal horn arrangement. There's straight-ahead jazz, and down-home blues, in 'Farewell To Old Friends', where the Hammond is at its most distinctive. It's the ballad 'Sweet Poison', though, that leaves the deepest mark, with distant echoes of Hancock in the opening melody and Zawinul in the solo, where the second harmonic percussion on the 888000000 drawbars adds a subtle touch. **Sound And Style 20, p148, CD track 37.**

In Dennerlein's ever expanding sound wardrobe, more recent additions have been church organ, on *Spiritual Movement No. 1* (2001), and symphony orchestra combined with Hammond, on *Change Of Pace* (2007), both on her Bebab label. The former harks all the way back to Fats Waller, even to the inclusion of 'Ain't Misbehavin'', and the latter calls to mind the symphonic excursions of British rockers Lord and Emerson.

Nothing could be further from the mind of Joey DeFrancesco, who is more than content to follow the master where the sound of the B-3 is concerned. If there is a touch of the evangelical about his pronouncements on the rights and wrongs of Hammond style and technique, it's only because he is very good at it. His hands seem to be moulded around the keys as he dips in and out of tonality with the ease of a graceful spider, not an ounce of tension in his hands or feet. The organ must be a very familiar piece of furniture to him though, having grown up at the feet of 'Papa' John DeFrancesco, an organist and trumpeter, who in turn had been weaned on jazz courtesy of his father Joe DeFrancesco, a big-band saxophonist who hailed from Sicily. Born in 1971 and brought up in Philadelphia – where else? – the young Joey DeFrancesco was surrounded by the sound of the B-3, and even though he learned piano, he was attracted to the organ as soon as his legs were long enough.

It's not every youngster who receives an invitation to work with Miles Davis, but Joey DeFrancesco found himself on a Davis album, playing 'additional' keyboards alongside George Duke on 'Cobra', from 1989's *Amandla*. The CD credits mention that "Joey DeFrancesco appears courtesy of CBS Records", and so he did, having signed a five-album deal while still in his teens. But what was he going to record?

"First time I saw him [Jimmy Smith] was in 1978," recalled DeFrancesco in a 2006 interview. "I was seven years old. It was New York City at the Sheraton. He wasn't playing a B-3. He was playing this German organ called a Wersi, which he was endorsing."[17] Strange that Jimmy Smith was playing a Wersi, but not strange that DeFrancesco was seemingly fixated by the experience, even analysing Smith's footwork when the lower manual went down, preventing Jimmy from playing the bass line with his left hand. DeFrancesco spent his school years absorbing organ wisdom. Not only did he have tuition with the greats, McDuff, Holmes, and Patterson, he invested time and perspiration listening to, transcribing, and re-creating the soul-jazz canon, particularly as represented in the works of Jimmy Smith.

IF THERE IS A TOUCH OF THE EVANGELICAL ABOUT JOEY DEFRANCESCO'S PRONOUNCEMENTS ON HAMMOND TECHNIQUE, IT'S BECAUSE HE'S GOOD AT IT.

So, to answer the question. Joey's first album, *All Of Me* (Columbia 1989), finds the organist in the midst of some expensive arrangements involving strings and horns, but the title track says it all in its relative simplicity, unflinching swing, and debt to Jimmy Smith. Guitarist John Scofield and tenor saxophonist Illinois Jacquet make an appearance on the next album, upping the star factor, but it's a few albums on that the trio of Joey, guitarist Pat Bollenback, and drummer Byron Landham comes of age, on 1992's *Reboppin'*. This, the fourth of the Columbia series, also includes Joey's brother Johnny on guitar and 'Papa John DeFrancesco, to keep it in the family; but the quality of the trio and the material mark this one out. Tunes by Horace Silver ('Sister Sadie'), Wayne Shorter ('E.S.P.'), and Thelonius Monk ('Evidence') stand beside originals from DeFrancesco and Bollenback. DeFrancesco reached world audiences by touring and recording with the guitarist John McLaughlin and The Free Spirits, featuring drummer Dennis Chambers, of whom more later. 1994's *After The Rain* featured Elvin Jones on drums, with a repertoire of mainly John Coltrane tunes.

The sound of the Hammond will not surprise you; innovation is not the point with Joey. What you get is an immense, instinctive knowledge of what really works on the B-3, BC, B-2, C-3, A-100, or any of the vast collection of tonewheel organs DeFrancesco owns. So for solos his setting is 888000000 with third-harmonic fast percussion, with options on the fourth and eighth drawbars for extra sparkle. Lower manual guidelines are 808000000 with an option on the 2 2/3' drawbar. Vibrato setting is the standard C3. Of course there are variations on this, as there are with note choice. It's tempting to think that his solo language was handed down from the prophets, but in fact modernity sits on top of the bed of soul jazz, providing more options in the chromatic alteration department.

To check this, fast forward to the album *The Champ* (High Note, 1999), which is a tribute to Smith, and specifically to the 'Organ Grinder's Swing', which shows what DeFrancesco can add to a replica of a theme. In the company of organ trio guitar specialist Randy Johnston and the ever-young Billy Hart on drums, the head – the opening tune – is pretty much note for note as in the Jimmy Smith version; and indeed the organ solo looks set for an imitative stance until the end of the second chorus. But then Joey executes the turnaround in thoroughly un-JS fashion, ripping through a maelstrom of 16th-notes, each perfectly articulated. More JS quotes follow, and the track ends rather strangely with a slightly clumsy registration change for the big finish. **Sound And Style 21, p150, CD track 38.**

Other tribute albums from DeFrancesco have continued to flow: *The Champ:Round 2* in 2000; *The Philadelphia Connection: A Tribute To Don Patterson* two years later; a Sinatra tribute two years after that. But it's the double B-3 albums with JS that have excited the Hammond fraternity in the 21st century. *Incredible* (2000) and *Legacy* (2005) are the sound of two ace Hammond players stepping round each other, with no treading on toes along the way, and enjoying each other's musical company. So it was in real life; the two hung out regularly together, and Smith describes the empathy between them: "The secret is listening. I'm up there, and Joey's up there, playing this intense shit, but the fact is, our ears are a lot busier than our fingers. A lot of people show up wanting to see one of us cut the other down, y'know, 'the battle of the B-3s.' You don't battle somebody you enjoy playing with this much."[18]

The list of musicians wanting to play with Larry Goldings must be as long as your arm by now. When a player's career starts with a year with singer Jon Hendricks, then three years with guitarist Jim Hall, you might suspect he could play a bit, and you'd be right. Born in 1968 in Boston, Larry studied piano and didn't take up the organ until drummer Leon Parker pleaded with him to do a gig at Augie's Club, later to become Smoke, in New York City. The bass player hadn't been able to make it, so Leon, knowing the strength of Larry's left-hand playing,

Larry Goldings: only too pleased to experiment.

called him up. Larry takes up the story: "I brought a DX7 up there, and essentially walked bass lines, and found a cheesy organ sound on the DX and finished out the gig that way, and that's how it all began because he ended up wanting me to play up there regularly."[19]

Not, you might say, an auspicious start, but the gig turned regular, very regular, and eventually evolved into a trio with Larry on Hammond, Peter Bernstein on guitar, and Bill Stewart on drums. Amongst the many strings to his bow, this trio highlights Larry's organ playing most effectively. With a string of well-received albums to its name, the trio is the musical situation in which Larry feels most comfortable. Starting in 1991 with *Intimacy Of The Blues*, on Verve, right up to *Sweet Science* in 2002, on the Palmetto label, the trio's output averaged an album a year. In the meantime, Goldings was hired by Maceo Parker, with whom he got the chance to explore the funk side of the Hammond, John Scofield, saxophonist Michael Brecker, guitarist Pat Metheny, and the singer-songwriter James Taylor.

Often cited as the natural heir to Larry Young, Goldings takes in the area of post-bebop as well as expanding outwards. The Larry Young connection continues in that Goldings, drummer Jack DeJohnette, and

> OFTEN CITED AS THE NATURAL HEIR TO LARRY YOUNG, LARRY GOLDINGS TAKES IN THE AREA OF POST-BEBOP AS WELL AS EXPANDING OUTWARDS.

Scofield have a group called Trio Beyond, which re-invigorates the work of Tony Williams' Lifetime. Incidentally, the Trio Beyond's record, *Saudades*, received a Jazz Grammy nomination in 2007.

Larry isn't afraid of using other keyboards to replicate Hammond behaviour: "My favourite non-Hammond to play is the Korg CX3 … that's the one I know the best. It's important to have a Leslie, and a volume pedal, and if the organ is the main focus of the group, then MIDI another keyboard to give you two keyboards."[20] When it comes to drawbar sound, the Jimmy Smith solo setting is the starting point, but if there is a bass player, thus a hand free, then Goldings is only too pleased to experiment: "I'm constantly trying to find some different sounds, and sometimes I randomly pull some out until I find something that sounds good!"[21] And good it does sound.

Returning to *Sweet Science*, the soundscape ranges from church-like on 'Chorale', to the blues on 'Solid Jack', to kitsch on 'This Guy's In Love With You'. New textures, voicings, and grooves abound: the ultra-high and intricate lines of

'Gnomesville', and the groovy but spare version of Rodgers and Hart's 'Spring Is Here', which boasts some subtle volume-pedal manipulation. Emphasis on fourths, in chord voicings as well as in solo lines, is evident, another throwback to Young. The opening track, 'Asimov', brings to mind the compositions of Carla Bley, jazz composer extraordinaire and erstwhile Hammond player, with whom Goldings recorded the album *4 X 4* in 2000. Bley herself grew up in church, as it were, switching to piano many decades later when Hammond duties were passed over to her daughter Karen Mantler, herself an accomplished player. Carla's playing is showcased on Steve Swallow's *Carla* (Watt Works, 1987), and Karen's attachment to the B-3 is amply illustrated on the track 'My Organ', from her 1990 Watt Works release *Get The Flu*, attributed to Karen Mantler And Her Cat Arnold. But back to Goldings; there's something of Bley's open and unrelated harmonic movement in 'Asimov', and there's also something of Scofield's penchant for inner part dissonance. **Sound And Style 22, p152, CD track 39.**

Larry Goldings' use of the Korg CX-3 is not unusual. Many players have switched to modern alternatives, sometimes reluctantly, but mostly because the tonewheel substitutes are much improved. Take Joey DeFrancesco, interviewed in 2006: "Actually about 99 per cent of the time I use new Hammond products.... They started making B-3s in '55 and they stopped in '75. And by '68, they got it so refined that they started to become very consistent with the sound. That's the sound everybody really loves and that's how the new B-3 sounds to me. Now, the new B-3 has real contacts in it. That's what makes it maybe a little better than the XK stuff that doesn't have mechanical contacts. The XK has the same type of generator, but the contacts aren't mechanical. And that mechanical contact just makes it feel like the real thing, you know?'[22]

At the time of writing, the Hammond range is in good shape. The XK-1 is a single manual, one set of drawbars, 61-note keyboard, with 'waterfall' keys with rounded edges that don't shred your hands, as used on the B-3, C-3, and A-100. The XK-3 has all this and more. The two sets of 96 independent digital tonewheels are accurate, there's a tube preamp to drive the overdrive, there are three sets of drawbars, and an opportunity not only to link any MIDI keyboard and pedals, but also to hook up an XLK-3, turning the whole thing into a two-manual organ. Fair enough, you don't get the mechanical click that DeFrancesco mentions. But you'd have to pay very serious money indeed for the massive 'New B-3', launched in 2003, that is the chief contender for faithful tonewheel reproduction.

How about the other half of the sound equation, the Leslie system? Although digital emulations of a Leslie are routinely provided in digital organs and synths, a dedicated Hammond player would want the physical rotating process on stage or in the studio. Since Leslie is now part of the Hammond Suzuki setup, the best and most infinitely flexible solution is a Leslie 2101 for the top end linked to a 2121 bass unit, delivering enough power to compete with, yes, even a guitar.

If your Hammond organ ambition doesn't stretch to owning and touring the 'real' thing, there are other options in the 'clonewheel' world that suit more occasional devotees of the B-3 spin.

Tonewheel sounds in the 21st century

Because the clonewheels are now so good, it has become well nigh impossible to separate the real from the not-so-real. In a sense, the source of the noise is of no importance to the listener unless there's something lacking. That's rarely the case nowadays, because from the first virtual models to the latest software emulations the versatility and sound quality have been consistently high. There will always be players who hanker for the real deal, and indeed by owning a clonewheel you are sacrificing the individuality and character of each particular tonewheel instrument, but the practical advantages are huge; and given the right model you can choose between a dirty or a clean B-3, a swampy A-100, and so on.

The two main contenders in the clonewheel stakes, aside from Hammond, have been the Korg and Roland organs. The Korg CX-3 dates back to 1979, when it became the benchmark in the field. In those days it was an analogue instrument, but with percussion, distortion and variable key click. (Apparently Keith Emerson came up with the idea of including that.) There is also the BX-3, a two-manual version of the instrument.

Roland's entry into the virtual modelling tonewheel organ market was the VK-7, now transformed into the dual manual VK-77 and single VK-8 with 'waterfall' keys and built-in 'Composite Object Sound Modelling' digital sound processing, so that the player can sculpt and tweak highs and lows, and warmth and cold, as well as recreating the sound of amplification pushed into overdrive. One of the few complaints concerning virtual tonewheels is the sound of a glissando; on the non-Hammonds, the individual pitches can be too distinct, whereas with a Hammond clone the gliss is more of a mush. Latest arrival on the clonewheel stage is the Clavia Nord C-1, which appears to have solved the problem of fitting a dual manual organ under your arm, plus providing a strong organ sound with all the required controls.

Should you have a plethora of keyboards to hand, and you don't mind ripping your palms to shreds with synth keys, maybe a hardware module would be more up your street, in which case the Voce V5 provides what may be the most authentic sounding Hammond around. The module provides one set of drawbars, three channels of MIDI for two manuals and pedals, all the click and vibrato and percussion switches, plus a tonewheel leakage control that attempts to replicate the imperfections of the B-3. The same company's Spin II captures a Leslie effect in a small box.

With many keyboard players moving their sound sources to laptop computer, either in software synths or samples, taking a keyboard controller or two and connecting by MIDI to a software instrument is another option. At the top end of the market is Native Instruments' B4 II, which basically allows the player to adjust any parameter imaginable, which is fine if you also have all the time imaginable to explore those parameters. If you don't, it includes presets that cover a wide range of styles.

If the top of the range is too prohibitive, there are other plug-ins available at little or no cost. The popular music software Logic has its own instrument, the EVB3, which according to most reports comes a close second to the B4, losing out only on warmth of sound. Other ways of making a Hammond sort of a noise? Most synths have Hammond samples built in, most have a rotary speaker effect, some even offer drawbar control using controllers. Some are more successful than others. The virtual modelling cards for Korg synths have interesting organ presets; not realistic, necessarily, but the realtime control makes them musical.

There is even a forum on the internet where discussions take place on the best way to configure nine sine waves in drawbar configuration. There is also a site where you can observe and admire the waveform of any drawbar setting. My favourite is 800000008, which looks like a millipede.[23]

With all these means of production at our disposal, what music is being played on Hammond organs and by whom?

There is a list as long as your drawbar-operating arm of musicians and writers who may not be specialist players but have included organ regularly in their arrangements. Organ sounds are peppered throughout the work of Prince, for instance, though not always played by him. Minneapolis keyboardist Ricky Peterson and the late Boni Boyer (for *Lovesexy*) both have Hammond credits, as do Morris Hayes and Rosie Gaines. It is not surprising that the organ sound has resonances for Prince; his great influence, James Brown, was also a Hammond aficionado. On 'Satisfied' from the 2006 album *3121*, there is a gospelly Hammond played by Prince himself, if the lack of credit is anything to go by. It's a 12/8 ballad and the organ sits perfectly behind voice and horns, with interesting things to say but in a low voice.

Donald Fagen is another who has consistently turned to the Hammond in both his solo records and with guitarist and co-writer Walter Becker in Steely Dan. From *Gaucho* to *Everything Must Go*, the Hammond finds its way into the tightly worked arrangements, though probably not as first choice. Fagen's customary modus operandi is to start tracks on Rhodes or piano then arrange outwards. But on Fagen's 1982 solo album, *The Nightfly*, one gets the feeling that the organ is more integral, perhaps because the lyrical concept has an eye on the 1950s and 1960s. Not only is it a classic album, it boasts some of Fagen's most prominent Hammond work, including the jaunty offbeat swing of 'Walk Between Raindrops'. Fagen reveals: "The organ at the studio where we were working was very funky-sounding, which is unusual. I think it was broken, which is probably why it sounds so good." [24]

From two acknowledged masters of the songwriting craft to two women songwriters who have espoused the B-3 in recent years: Sheryl Crow and Tori Amos. Crow's use of the Hammond dates back to 1996 and the *Sheryl Crow* album, where its arrival on 'Hard To Make A Stand' is announced by a strong riff, reminiscent of 'Gimme Some Lovin''. Meanwhile Amos's 2005 release, *The Beekeeper*, is dripping with the honey of the B, as it were. The B-3, a Christmas present from her husband, has changed Amos' sound world. The best Hammond track is 'Witness'; the playing is textural, but evocative none the less.

In pop circles, interest in the Hammond continues. Take The Kaiser Chiefs and their keyboardist Peanut, also known as Nick Baines, who is stuck on the real deal: "I was playing these really long notes, and my whole body was shaking from the Leslie which was sat next to me. It's that kind of power in the sound, makes you feel good." [25] The track in question is 'I Predict A Riot' from the band's 2004 debut album *Employment*.

In the USA, jazz organ is alive and well in the hands of Sam Yahel. He has four albums under his belt, the last of which, *Truth And Beauty*, has attracted positive reviews, including this from the *New York Times*: "This record overcomes old organ-and-tenor jazz clichés so easily that you hardly think of them. The music is fluid, flexible, all parts running together, the groove overwhelming." [26] Helping to supply that groove is drummer Brian Blade, and Joshua Redman is the tenor player.

At the other end of the spectrum is another US-based group, Niacin, barely

Tori Amos (top); Sam Yahel (below).

CLASSIC HAMMOND ORGAN – **THE PLAYERS**

containing organist John Novello, drummer Dennis Chambers, and bassist Billy Sheehan. They are a great example to finish on, because they embrace, or rather devour, the complete history of anything anyone's ever played on a B-3 or the like; Jimmy Smith and soul-jazz are there, Emerson is definitely there, Winwood is there, all supercharged by tight, energetic, and above all musical playing. Sheehan remembers: "[The Hammond] is a really distinguishable sound, and for a long time, I remember, in the late '60s and the early '70s, if you didn't have a B-3, you were basically out of luck as a band. Everybody had to have one. It was as integral a part of the music in that era as the Telecaster, Strat, Les Paul, Fender P-bass or Ludwig drums."[27] And it continues to be so. In whatever form it may take – a wooden cabinet, a plastic keyboard driving a module, a window on a laptop – the Hammond tonewheel sound is not about to go away. For an instrument that looked to be a replacement for the pipe organ, the B-3 has carved a career for itself that has taken many unexpected turns, thanks to the varied roster of gifted musicians who took it up and made it their instrument of choice.

'THE HAMMOND IS A REALLY DISTINGUISHABLE SOUND, AND FOR A LONG TIME, I REMEMBER, IF YOU DIDN'T HAVE A B-3 YOU WERE OUT OF LUCK AS A BAND.'

Footnotes

[1] Obituary of Count Basie by John S. Wilson, *New York Times* April 27th 1984.

[2] *Miles: The Autobiography*, by Miles Davis with Quincy Troupe

[3] *Talking That Talk: Le Langage Du Blues Et Du Jazz*, by Jean-Paul Levet

[4] Interview with Jimmy Smith and John DeFrancesco, by Stephen Fortner, *Keyboard* magazine, February 2005

[5] *Keyboard* magazine, February 2005

[6] *Keyboard* magazine, February 2005

[7] *Keyboard* magazine, February 2005

[8] Quoted in *Beauty And The B*, by Mark Vail

[9] Auger, quoted by Lois Wilson in the liner notes to *Streetnoise* (Sanctuary Records)

[10] Interviewed by Clemens Steenweg for *Classic Rock Start Page* (www.classicrock-startpage.com/mannfredmanninterview.html), October 2002

[11] Quoted in 'Spencer Davis Group' on *Brum Beat* (www.brumbeat.net/sdgroup.htm)

[12] Transcription of press conference at Hell railway station, Norway, on September 19th 2003, by Rasmus Heide (www.picturedwithin.com/tour/hell/pressconf.html)

[13] Quoted in *Beauty And The B*, by Mark Vail

[14] *The Culture Show*, BBC2, Hammond 70th birthday item

[15] Interview by Mike Brannon for *All About Jazz*, April 1999 (www.allaboutjazz.com/iviews/jmedeski.htm)

[16] Interviewed by Steve Lodder, November 2007

[17] Interviewed by Michael Gallant, *Keyboard* magazine, July 2006

[18] 'Jimmy And Joey's Excellent Adventure' by Stephen Fortner, *Keyboard* magazine, February 2005

[19] Interviewed by Steve Lodder, November 2007

[20] Interviewed by Steve Lodder, November 2007

[21] Interviewed by Steve Lodder, November 2007

[22] Interviewed by Michael Gallant, *Keyboard* magazine, July 2006

[23] Tim Wick's Hammond drawbar wave simulation (http://theatreorgans.com/hammond/drawbar.htm)

[24] *High Fidelity* magazine, January 1983

[25] *The Culture Show*, BBC2, Hammond 70th birthday item

[26] Ben Ratcliff, *New York Times*, Top Ten of 2007

[27] Official website of Niacin (www.niacinb3.com)

Billy Preston (above) was a child prodigy who went on to play
Hammond on The Beatles' *Let It Be* album. Brian Auger (top right)
set himself the task of creating a bridge between jazz and rock.
Shirley Scott (bottom right) started on piano but her career took
off when she switched to Hammond in the mid 1950s.

Classic Hammond

THE
MUSIC

THIS SECTION consists of two sets of musical examples. The first set, 'Examples', is intended to provide a taster of the range of Hammond organ styles. The second set, called 'Sound And Style', deals with individual musicians; the examples are not transcriptions of themes or solos, but indications of their writing and playing, inspired by the particular track mentioned in the 'Players' section above. Sometimes these are close to the original, sometimes they are more inventive.

Never feel you can't experiment with the sounds. The suggested registrations are a starting point only, and whether you're playing a drawbar organ, a preset keyboard with no split facilities or the latest bells-and-whistles computer emulation, the ear is always the final arbiter of good sound choice. Your settings define your personal style, so while it's perfectly fine to start with imitation, work your way into an individual sound world. Of course, certain things about the instrument just work with no frills; the classic sounds are classic for a good reason.

It might be that you are a rock player with little interest in jazz, or a jazz aficionado with a distaste for rock, or even a lounge player with no interest in anything else save for the organ bossa novas of Brazilian Walter Wanderley, in which case you might be tempted to skip past examples in an alien style. My advice would be to stick with the programme and try to widen your range of musical environments, because you never know where it might lead.

■ Descriptions of sounds, where appropriate, use the standard drawbar arrangement with U for Upper and L for Lower manual. Drawbar settings are normally annotated using numbers in a row: **888888888**, for instance, would mean that every stop was on maximum.

■ The vibrato dial is set to C3 unless otherwise stated; similarly Leslie is set to chorale/slow or off and vibrato is off as a starting point. Percussion is normal volume and fast decay unless otherwise indicated.

■ The exercises are not progressive in difficulty, so if you have problems with notation or execution, it might be sensible to work through the more rock/soul/reggae-based examples and then proceed to the trickier solo styles.

■ The basic hand position is with curved fingers and the thumb swinging under freely to change hand position. Try and find some video footage of Joey DeFrancesco for a guide to technique; there are some good examples on YouTube at the time of writing.

■ Pedal parts are included for those with the real instrument. Otherwise, play the pedal part with the left hand on the lower manual where practical. Your right foot should be on the volume pedal and left foot over the pedals or propped. Pedal notes are all executed with the left foot. Pedal drawbars are normally set to 16′, but with an option to include 8′ where needed. Note that the more 8′ in the sound the more intrusive and honky rather than supportive the sound.

■ Keyboard splits are easy to set up if you have just the one keyboard. Make sure the pitch is correct at the top end; organ sounds do sound a bit strange if they go above C5.

Grace-notes

The important grace-notes are mostly notated, but in the recorded examples you will hear additional inflections that would make the page hard to read if written exactly. The rule of thumb is always to add more; grace-notes are one of the prime means of inflection at an organist's disposal. What's even better is that if you brush a key unintentionally on the way to another, it's just another expressive gesture, not a mistake.

examples

EX 1: blues in C CD TRACK 1

One of the primary skills of an organist is playing a walking bass on the lower manual, if not on the pedals. The C blues is a good form to kick off with; play each hand separately at first and then combine them. After a while, try playing a solo over an improvised walking line.

U888000000/L808000000 percussion: third

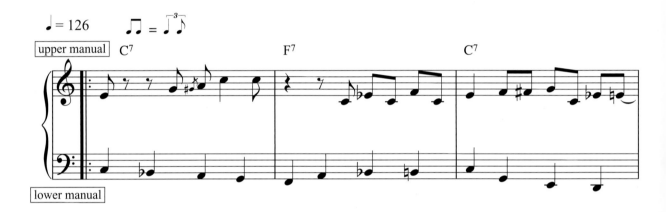

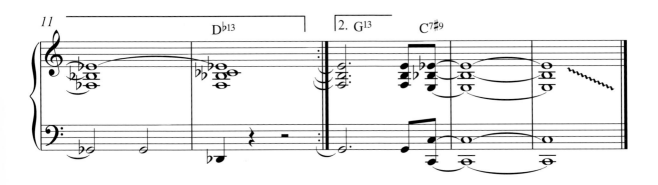

EX 2: blues in F CD TRACK 2

The F blues is the cornerstone of the jazz B-3 repertoire. Here there are some bebop-influenced lines, whereas the C blues was more soul-jazz; and harmonically this example is more developed. Bars eight and 12 use a tritone substitution at the end of the bar, which gives the bass line its classic shape. (A tritone substitution is where the root note of a chord is replaced with one three whole tones away: eg, G7 becomes D♭7. Normally the fifth and the ninth will be sharpened or flattened to ease the process. Here D7♭5 becomes A♭7♭5 and C7♯9♭13 becomes G♭7/9/13.) The flat fifth in the melody line in bars nine and ten stretches the harmony and provides a more angular top line.

U888000000/L808000000 percussion: third

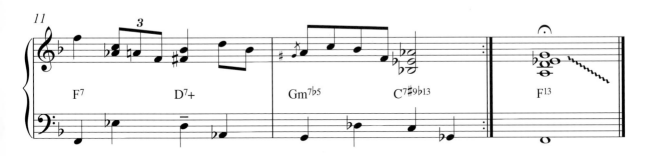

EX 3: blues in F, right-hand comping CD TRACK 3

Using the same form and left hand as Example 2, this exercise illustrates the kind of comping that might work with an F blues. The right-hand part is the sort of part that could be played under another instrument's solo, if there is one. Equally, it could be transferred to the left hand if there is a bass player, or left out completely if there is a guitarist comping. This is obviously a static part, there being no solo, and only ears can dictate how much flexibility it would need in a live situation.

L808000000

EX 4: rock in G CD TRACK 4

Getting used to glissandi and fistfuls of right-hand notes is all part of the rock brief; and enjoy the second time round when the Leslie starts whirling for the full ensemble effect.

U888868660/L808643000 percussion: second

EX 5: rock in A CD TRACK 5

An exercise firstly in moving three-note chords around the keys, and then, in the closing section, oscillating the hand around A7 and D9 shapes. Achieving the melodic line in bars one to four involves inversions of the basic chord, A major, and passing chords of D.

U888764400/L848800000 percussion: second

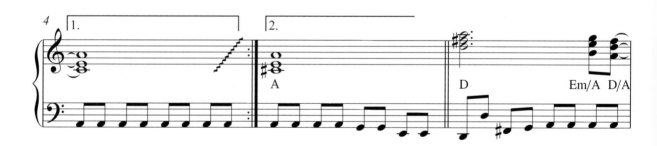

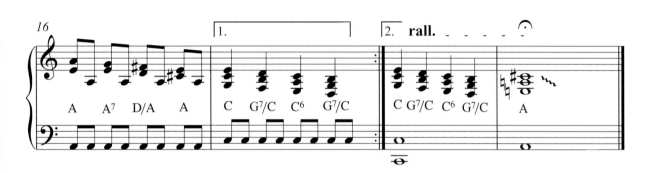

EX 6: funk CD TRACK 6

The D7$\sharp$9 chord contains both major and minor thirds (F-sharp and F), a major seventh apart, but mediated by the seventh in between (C). Funk voicings are generally more open, built on fourths and fifths rather than the close thirds of rock chords. Right-hand/left-hand interplay is crucial also, giving the rhythm a kick, as in bar 14 onwards. The device in bar seven of dipping a semitone and back again is borrowed from guitarists.

U888000000/L808000000 percussion: third

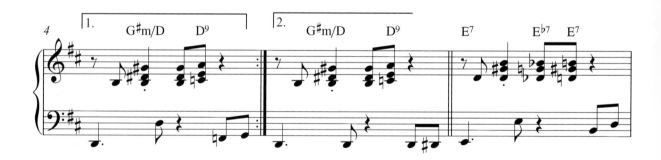

EX 7: jazz 3/4 CD TRACK 7

In this 3/4 groove, the harmony is derived from the 'standards' repertoire, with a further-reaching harmonic palette and some surprise twists. The pedal part is included to provide a co-ordination exercise for those lucky enough to have that option. Less difficult than a walking line, it's a fairly gentle way in.

U888000000/L837000000 percussion: second

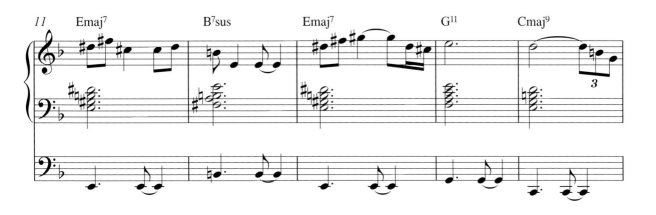

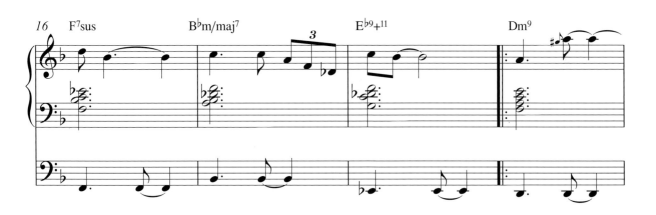

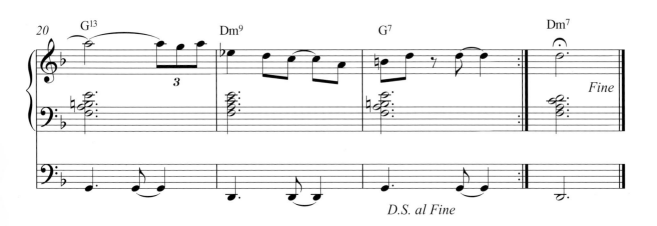

EX 8: soul/motown CD TRACK 8

An echo of soul/Motown themes here; the voicings have closed up again in the right hand, and the syncopation is crucial. It's also refreshing to be able to use major seventh and major ninth chords without a guilty conscience.

U600403000/L808000000

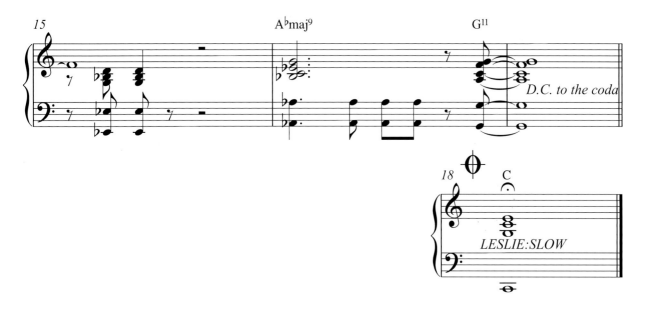

EX 9: repeated notes CD TRACK 9

The stuttering so common in 1960s jazz takes a while to get smooth. Don't attempt it on a weighted keyboard; only a Hammond or a synth will be fast enough. The fingering suggested here is personal; there are other ways, no doubt, so try your own.

U888000000/L808000000 percussion: third

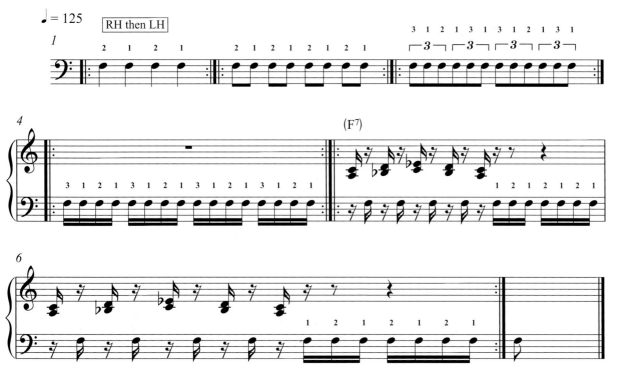

EX 10: held top note CD TRACK 10

This can be a fair stretch for the fingers, so approach with care. It provides a smooth way of changing chords, supplying inner movement but sustained texture.

U888000000

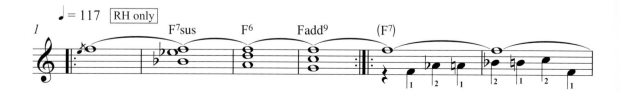

LESLIE FAST

EX 11: switching manuals CD TRACK 11

Set the upper manual to 16′ and the lower manual to 8′ and the result is an interesting change of octave, helping you get familiar with the spaces between the two manuals.

U800000000/L008000000

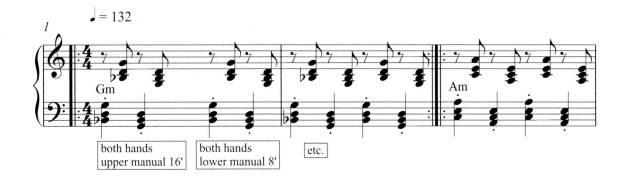

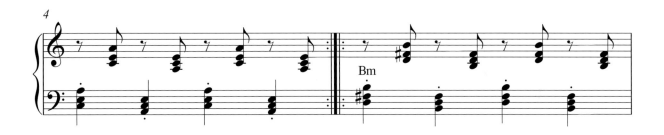

EX 12: preset with effect CD TRACK 12

Changing presets (the black keys to the left of the manual) in a groove can animate a static chord where you want some movement and you want to draw attention to yourself. The preset keys can be a bit clunky, so spare a thought for the instrument.

LH: change black key presets as indicated in lower stave

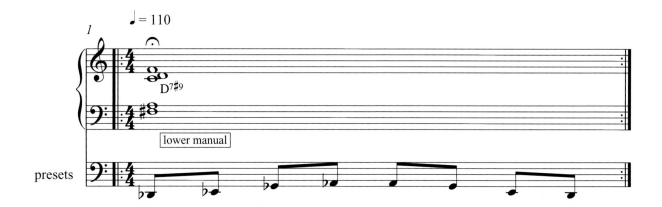

EX 13: mystic drawbars CD TRACK 13

Here the right hand is sustaining the chords, the left hand is pulling bars, and the pedal is keeping the time.

LH: pull drawbars pedals 84

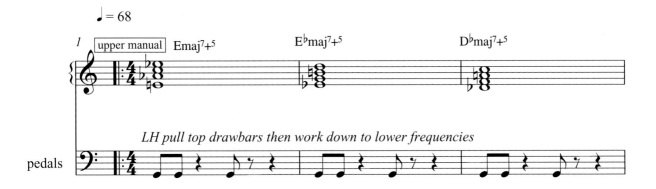

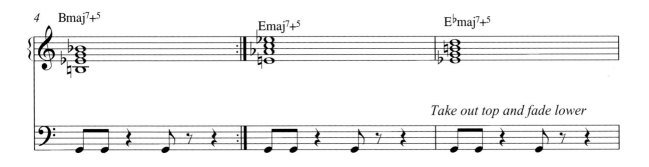

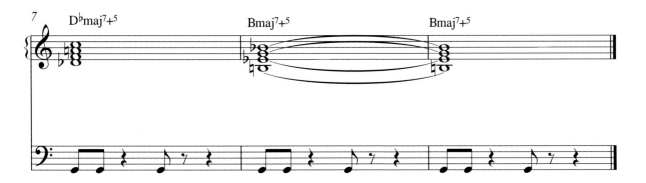

EX 14: dodging the rain CD TRACK 14

This is a 'skank' in the style of Donald Fagen, the bass walking very carefully between drops of rain.

U807030000/L867000000

EX 15: two-hand block chord voicings CD TRACK 15

For a big band emulation, voice the right with seventh chords and double the top line an octave down with the left hand. A ninth between left hand and right hand also works well.

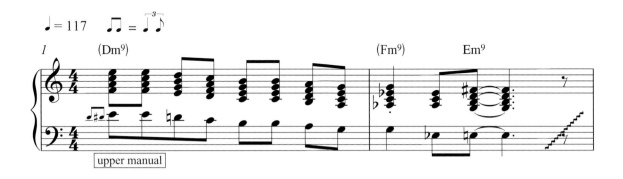

EX 16: expression control CD TRACK 16

This is about volume pedal, Leslie switching, and vibrato switching. Your right foot is firmly on the expression pedal, and your left hand is free to toggle vibrato and Leslie when there is the brain space to think about it.

U660000045/L703424700

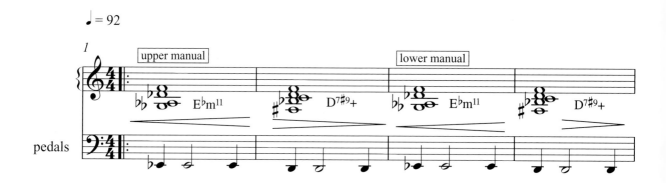

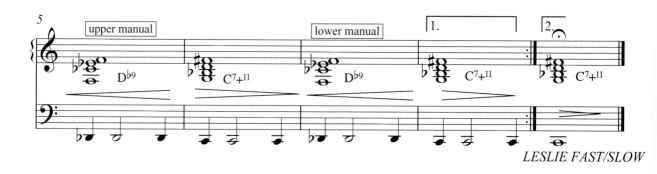

LESLIE FAST/SLOW

sound and style examples

S&S 1: JIMMY SMITH CD TRACK 17

Play with a standard JS registration. The clash in bar three between the A and the implied seventh of the chord, A-flat, is taken from the source.

U888000000   percussion: third

S&S 2: JACK MCDUFF CD TRACK 18

The sound here should be as squelchy as possible, honey dripping from every note, and the thirds as smooth as fingers can execute.

U840000088 percussion: third, Leslie fast, vibrato on

S&S 3: JIMMY MCGRIFF CD TRACK 19

This is a good place to practise the tremolo in bars one and four and the speed of a repeated pattern in bar six.

U888444000 percussion: third, overdriven

S&S 4: RICHARD 'GROOVE' HOLMES CD TRACK 20

The equivalent of saying "six thistle sticks" over and over, Holmes's sixteenth-notes are a thing of great wonder. It's another chance to practise those spitting repeated notes.

U888000008   no percussion (that disables the 1′ stop)

S&S 5: DR LONNIE SMITH CD TRACK 21

Keeping the groove going while playing the sixteenth-notes in bar seven is a little tricky; just get the left hand running in semi-automatic mode.

U888800000/L808000000

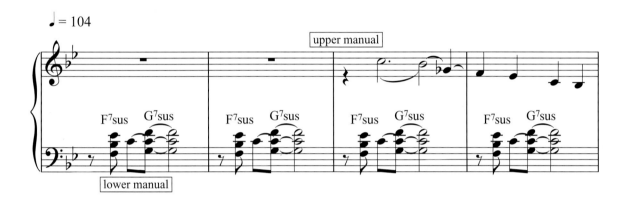

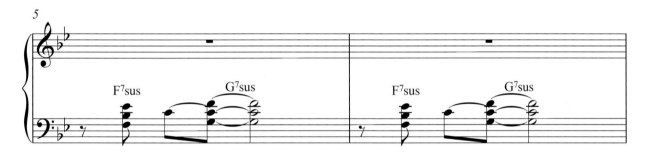

S&S 6: SHIRLEY SCOTT CD TRACK 22

Several things to look out for here: the percussion phrasing of the melody, breaking the phrase according to taste, and the pedal line, where I cheated by playing left-hand chords and bass on the lower manual and overdubbing the top line.

U508600000/L007000000 percussion: second

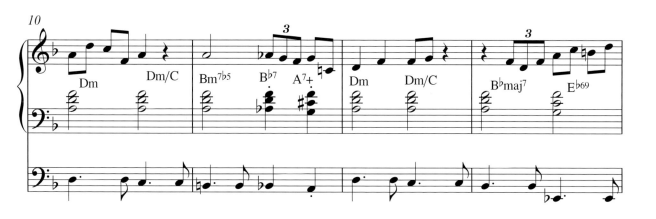

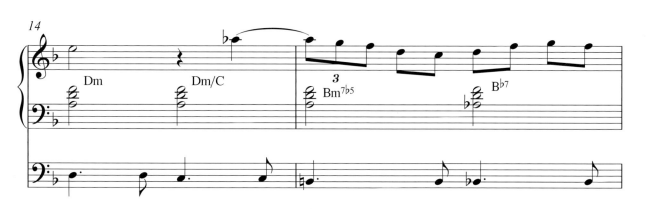

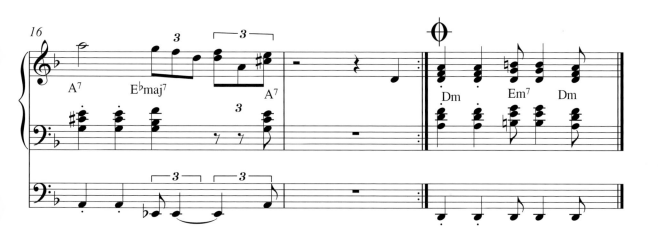

S&S 7: LARRY YOUNG CD TRACK 23

Young's interest in the interval of a fourth is illustrated here, as well as his inclination to use scale passages when soloing. Experiment with foot volume control; Young uses it very carefully. If you are an infrequent Hammond player, volume pedal control is the one thing that might give you away; it's a relationship between foot and brain that takes time to develop. With experience, it's possible to set the overall level to about 75 per cent and then use the last 25 per cent to kick in a higher level where you want a strong accent. This is what Young does extensively; foot to the floor and immediately flick back to the lower level again. To try this out, lean into the two quarter-notes in bars 9 and 11, re-establishing normal volume for the ending.

U888800000 percussion: third, soft

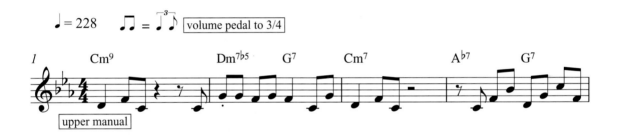

S&S 8: BOOKER T. JONES CD TRACK 24

This exercise is not designed to be played together. Play the lower-manual part first to get the feel of the riff, then play the top line, adding a left-hand part when possible. I overdubbed the top line on the two-handed riff.

U858000000/L008761000

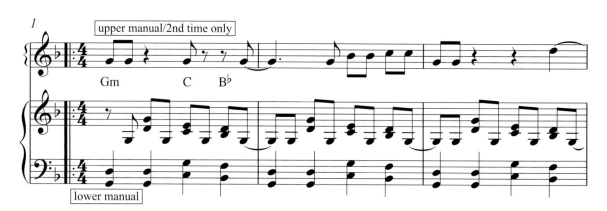

S&S 9: BILLY PRESTON CD TRACK 25

If this looks like a case of "play as many notes as you can with one hand", you'd be right. Make the final glissando as flat-palmed as possible for that engine-roar effect. Volume is at the player's discretion, but discreet is not it at all; maximise drama at every turn.

U658848446/L008807005 vibrato on both manuals

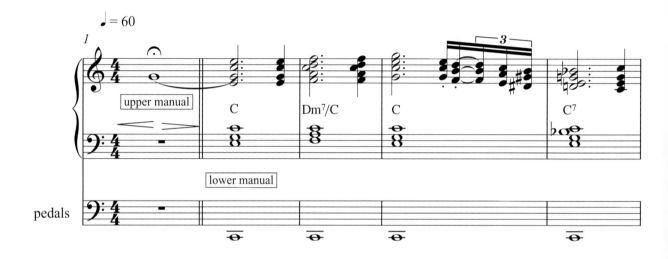

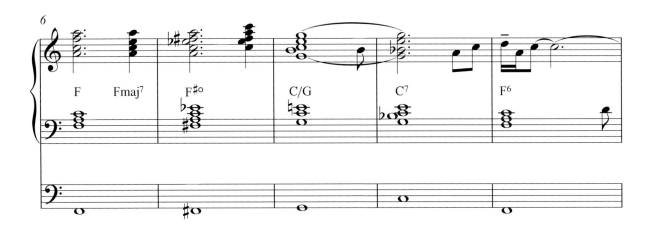

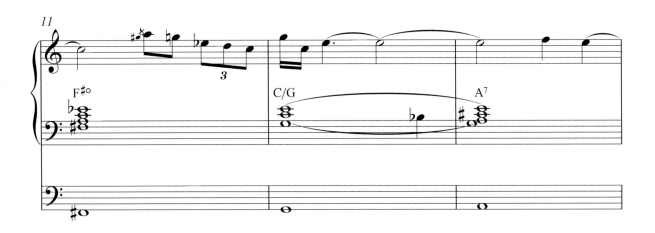

S&S 10: BRIAN AUGER CD TRACK 26

This gives an idea of the Dorian mode (white notes D-D), adding a flat fifth; in this case it's E minor with a B-flat.

U888866000 overdriven

S&S 11A: STEVE WINWOOD CD TRACK 27

The sound is fairly crunched, driving the Leslie hard, and each right-hand chord should have either an inner or top grace-note to achieve a suitable level of 'splurge'. The example uses many more keys than the original: it's good for you.

U888604442/L877600000 vibrato on

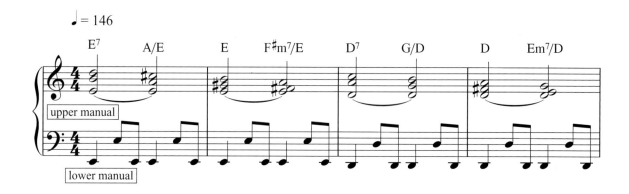

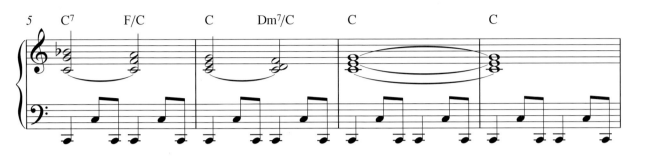

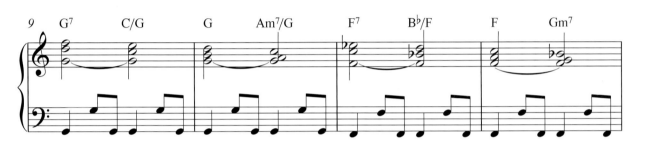

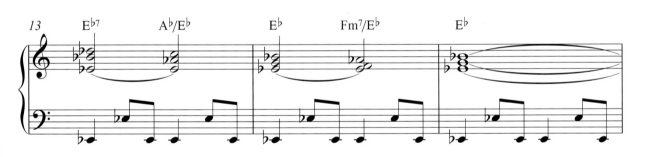

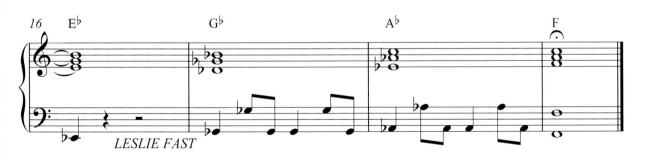

LESLIE FAST

S&S 11B: STEVE WINWOOD WITH HENDRIX CD TRACK 28

This might look intimidating, but once you hear it you realise that it makes more sense to the ear than the eye. The bottom line can be either left hand or feet, the latter leaving the left hand free for Leslie control.

U888000000/L848000000

S&S 12: JON LORD CD TRACK 29

Useful for getting a few 'stretched' notes – notes out of the immediate scale – under the fingers. Check the effect of the penultimate bar for dissonance/resolution.

U888400000 percussion: third, slow

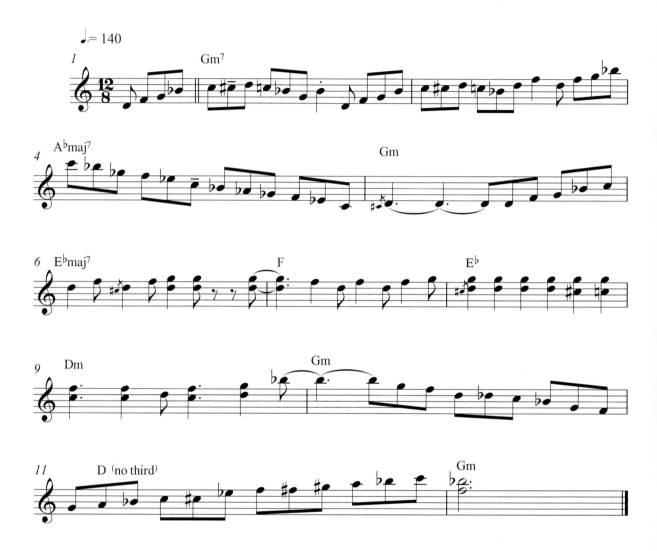

S&S 13: MATTHEW FISHER CD TRACK 30

Faithful to the original Procol Harum number in harmonic language and direction of line, but not, I hope, close enough to be taken to court.

U688800000/L008855000

S&S 14: KEITH EMERSON CD TRACK 31

The accompaniment is just for illustration to underpin the solo style, reduce to one hand if your left hand is pining for something to do. Maximum keyclick is required to achieve that Emerson aggression.

U888000000/L008080000 percussion: third, overdriven

LESLIE FAST

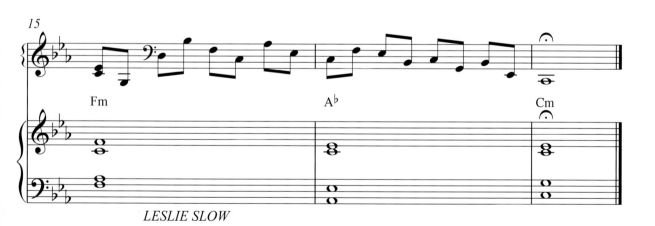

LESLIE SLOW

S&S 15: ROD ARGENT CD TRACK 32

Based on the first part of the solo in 'Hold Your Head Up'. The two lines weave around each other in a rare case of counterpoint in 1960s rock. Trying to keep the pedals steady while playing two independent parts is tricky but worth pursuing if you have them. It is also possible to play both parts in the right while left hand plays bass, except in bar nine, where you would need to release the low D.

U888000000 percussion: second, overdriven

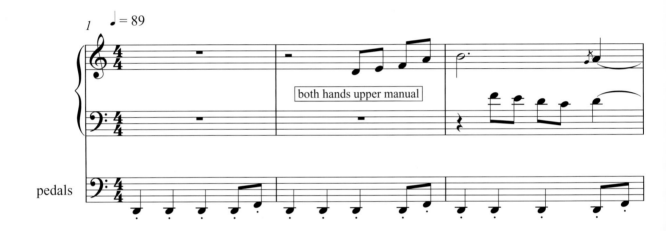

S&S 16: GREGG ROLIE CD TRACK 33

The chords remain the same throughout, and the chopping is worth a look in bars nine to 12; it's definitely an energy-provoking device. Once you've played it with your right hand on the beat, try reversing so your left hand is on.

U888804220 vibrato on

S&S 17: BERNARD HARVEY CD TRACK 34

This one is self-explanatory. Make sure the quavers are good and short, with maybe the right hand being slightly longer than the left, and that the whole style is laid-back and relaxed.

U B:688885060/B♭:008500666 L005000044

S&S 18: JAMES TAYLOR CD TRACK 35

An illustration of the filmic theme and acid jazz turnarounds. It shouldn't prove too challenging.

U888000556

S&S 19: JOHN MEDESKI CD TRACK 36

Less of a musical challenge, more of a mechanical one; the idea here is to find enough thinking space to operate the drawbars and presets, playing with the sound the way Medeski does.

U B:005300000/B♭:005300044 L506000000 percussion: third

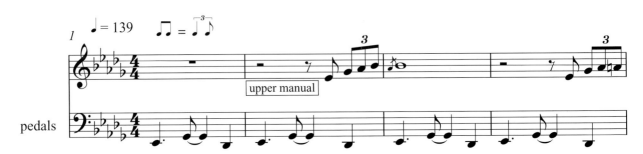

S&S 20: BARBARA DENNERLEIN CD TRACK 37

Many organ players reserve their feet for ballads. Not so Dennerlein; her footwork is as smart as her chord changes, which give the right hand an opportunity to anticipate the next chord change with some surprise choices of note.

U888000000/L008080000 percussion: second

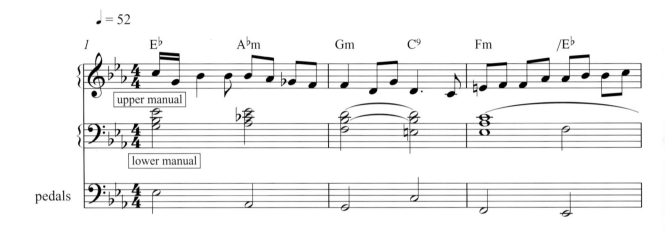

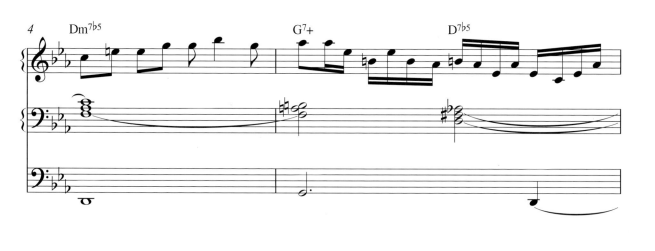

S&S 21: JOEY DEFRANCESCO CD TRACK 38

Taking what Jimmy Smith left as a starting point, Joey DeFrancesco expands the harmony, melodic line, and rhythmic subtlety. All this would be useless without a technique to match. Fortunately he has it in bucket-loads. What seems to start conventionally here soon turns nasty. If the right hand isn't enough of a challenge, comp with the left hand, walk with the pedals, and figure out what's wrong with the theory of relativity.

U888040000 percussion: third

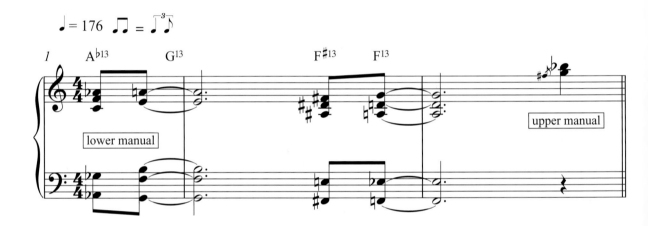

S&S 22: LARRY GOLDINGS CD TRACK 39

There's a freshness to Goldings' style that I hope is depicted here. A sense of surprise is present but no melodrama, with slightly stark left-hand voicings setting up the right-hand melody.

U888202660/L008000000 percussion: third

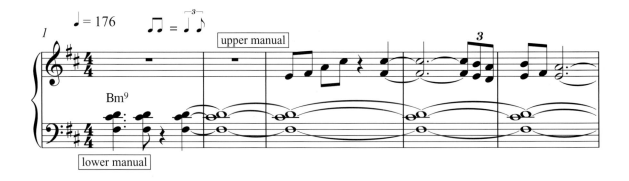

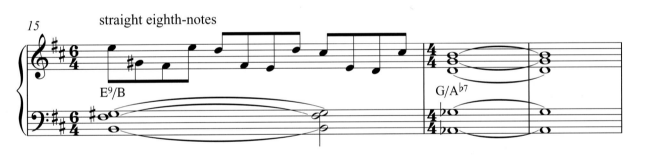

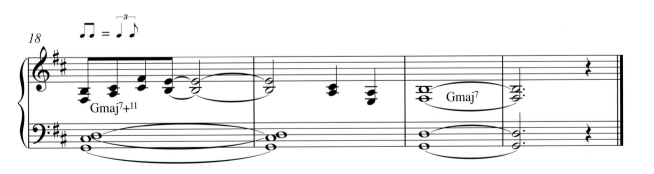

On the CD

The music on the CD was mainly recorded on a Hammond A-100 with a very funky keyclick, linked to a Leslie 122 speaker. Some examples were re-created on the very flexible Native Instruments B4II software clonewheel. No, I'm not telling; see if you can tell which is which.

CD TRACK 1 Example 1: blues in C

CD TRACK 2 Example 2: blues in F

CD TRACK 3 Example 3: blues in F, right-hand comping

CD TRACK 4 Example 4: rock inG

CD TRACK 5 Example 5: rock in A

CD TRACK 6 Example 6: funk

CD TRACK 7 Example 7: jazz 3/4

CD TRACK 8 Example 8: soul/motown

CD TRACK 9 Example 9: repeated notes

CD TRACK 10 Example 10: held top note

CD TRACK 11 Example 11: switching manuals

CD TRACK 12 Example 12: preset with effect

CD TRACK 13 Example 13: mystic drawbars

CD TRACK 14 Example 14: dodging the rain

CD TRACK 15 Example 15: two-hand block chord voicings

CD TRACK 16 Example 16: expression control

CD TRACK 17 Sound and style 1: Jimmy Smith

CD TRACK 18 Sound and style 2: Jack McDuff

CD TRACK 19 Sound and style 3: Jimmy McGriff

CD TRACK 20 Sound and style 4: Richard 'Groove' Holmes

CD TRACK 21 Sound and style 5: Dr Lonnie Smith

CD TRACK 22 Sound and style 6: Shirley Scott

CD TRACK 23 Sound and style 7: Larry Young

CD TRACK 24 Sound and style 8: Booker T. Jones

CD TRACK 25 Sound and style 9: Billy Preston

CD TRACK 26 Sound and style 10: Brian Auger

CD TRACK 27 Sound and style 11a: Steve Winwood

CD TRACK 28 Sound and style 11b: Steve Winwood with Jimi Hendrix

CD TRACK 29 Sound and style 12: Jon Lord

CD TRACK 30 Sound and style 13: Matthew Fisher

CD TRACK 31 Sound and style 14: Keith Emerson

CD TRACK 32 Sound and style 15: Rod Argent

CD TRACK 33 Sound and style 16: Gregg Rolie

CD TRACK 34 Sound and style 17: Bernard Harvey

CD TRACK 35 Sound and style 18: James Taylor

CD TRACK 36 Sound and style 19: John Medeski

CD TRACK 37 Sound and style 20: Barbara Dennerlein

CD TRACK 38 Sound and style 21: Joey DeFrancesco

CD TRACK 39 Sound and style 22: Larry Goldings

Recommended listening

The Allman Brothers, featuring Greg Allman
At Fillmore East (Capricorn)
Eat A Peach (Capricorn)

Tori Amos
The Beekeeper (Epic)

Argent, featuring Rod Argent
All Together Now (Epic)

Atomic Rooster, featuring Vince Crane
In Hearing Of Atomic Rooster (Pegasus)

Brian Auger's Oblivion Express
Brian Auger's Oblivion Express (Polydor, Disconforme)
Second Wind (RCA)

Brian Auger & The Trinity
Open (Atco)

Definitely What! (Atco)
Streetnoise (Polydor, Castle Music)
This Wheel's On Fire: The Best Of Brian Auger
  (Castle Music)

Count Basie
Count At The Organ (Verve)
Verve Jazz Masters Vol. 2

Blood, Sweat & Tears, featuring Al Kooper
Child Is The Father To The Man (Columbia)

Booker T. and the MGs
Green Onions (Stax)

The Brand New Heavies
The Brand New Heavies (Delicious Vinyl)

The Crazy World Of Arthur Brown, featuring Vince Crane
The Crazy World Of Arthur Brown (Track)

The Spencer Davis Group, featuring Steve Winwood
Their First LP (Fontana)
The Second Album (Fontana)

Wild Bill Davis
The Everest Years (Empire Music Werks)

Deep Purple, featuring Jon Lord
The Book Of Taliesyn (Parlophone/Tetragrammoton)
Concerto For Group And Orchestra
  (Harvest/Tetragrammoton)
Deep Purple In Rock (Harvest)
Machine Head (Purple, Warner Bros)

Joey DeFrancesco
All Of Me (Columbia)
Reboppin' (Columbia)
After The Rain (Verve)
The Champ (High Note)
The Champ: Round 2 (High Note)
*The Philadelphia Connection: A Tribute To Don
  Patterson* (High Note)

Joey DeFrancesco with Jimmy Smith
Incredible! (Concord)
Legacy (Concord)

Barbara Dennerlein
Straight Ahead (Enja)
Outhipped (Verve)
Change Of Pace (Bebab)

Bob Dylan, featuring Al Kooper
Highway 61 Revisited (Columbia)

Emerson Lake & Palmer, featuring Keith Emerson
Emerson Lake & Palmer (Island, Rhino)
Trilogy (Island, Rhino)
Pictures At An Exhibition (Island, Rhino)
Tarkus (Island, Rhino)

The Larry Goldings Trio
Intimacy Of The Blues (Verve)
Sweet Science (Palmetto)

The Grateful Dead, featuring Tom Constanten
Live Dead (Warner Bros)

Jimi Hendrix, featuring Steve Winwood
Electric Ladyland (Track, Reprise)

Richard 'Groove' Holmes
Groove (Pacific Jazz)
Welcome Home (Pacific Jazz)
Groovin' With Jug (Pacific Jazz)
Spicy (Prestige)
On Basie's Bandstand (Prestige)

Mahalia Jackson, featuring Billy Preston
The Best of Mahalia Jackson (Legacy/Columbia)

Led Zeppelin, featuring John Paul Jones
Led Zeppelin II (Atlantic)
Led Zeppelin III (Atlantic)
Physical Graffiti (Swan Song)

Little Feat, featuring Bill Payne
Time Loves A Hero (Warner Bros)

Karen Mantler And Her Cat Arnold
Get The Flu (XtraWATT)

Bob Marley & The Wailers, featuring Bernard 'Touter' Harvey
Natty Dread (Island)
Live! (Island)

Bob Marley & The Wailers, featuring Jean Alain Roussel
Natty Dread (Island)
Rastaman Vibration (Island)

Bob Marley & The Wailers, featuring John 'Rabbit' Bundrick
Catch A Fire (Island)

Brother Jack McDuff
Tough Duff (Prestige)
The Honeydripper (Prestige)

Jimmy McGriff
I've Got A Woman (Sue, Collectables)
The Worm (Blue Note)
Pullin' Out the Stops! The Best of Jimmy McGriff (EMI)

Jimmy McGriff and Richard 'Groove' Holmes
Giants Of The Organ In Concert (LRC)

Medeski Martin & Wood, featuring John Medeski
Combustication (Blue Note)

Medeski Scofield Martin & Wood, featuring John Medeski
Out Louder (Indirecto)

The Meters, featuring Art Neville
The Meters (Josie, Rhino)
The Original Funkmasters (Charly)

The Nice, featuring Keith Emerson
The Thoughts of Emerlist Davjack (Immediate)
Five Bridges (Charisma)
Elegy (Charisma)

Don Patterson, Booker Ervin,
Legends Of Acid Jazz (Prestige)

Pink Floyd, featuring Rick Wright
The Piper At The Gates Of Dawn (Columbia/EMI, Tower)

Billy Preston
The Most Exciting Organ Ever (Vee Jay)
That's The Way God Planned It (Apple)
Encouraging Words (Apple)
I Wrote A Simple Song (A&M)
Everybody Likes Some Kind Of Music (A&M)
The Collection (Purple Pyramid)
Billy's Bag (X5 Music Group)

Procol Harum, featuring Matthew Fisher
'A Whiter Shade Of Pale' (Deram)
Procol Harum (Deram)

Paul Quinichette, featuring Count Basie
The Complete Paul Quinichette (Blue Moon)
Partially issued on *The Vice 'Pres'* (Verve)

Santana, featuring Greg Rolie
Santana (Columbia)

Santana, featuring Tom Coster
Caravanserai (Columbia)
Moonflower (CBS)

John Scofield, featuring John Medeski
A Go Go (Verve)

Rhoda Scott & Kenny Clarke
Rhoda Scott & Kenny Clarke (Gitanes)

Shirley Scott
Great Scott (Prestige)

Shirley Scott & Clark Terry
Soul Duo (Impulse!)

Sly & The Family Stone
Dance To The Music (Epic)

Jimmy Smith
A New Sound, A New Star: Jimmy Smith At The Organ Vols. 1 and 2 (Blue Note)
The Incredible Jimmy Smith At The Organ (Blue Note)
The Incredible Jimmy Smith At Club Baby Grand Vols. 1 and 2 (Blue Note)
The Sermon! (Blue Note)
Back At The Chicken Shack (Blue Note)
Bashin': The Unpredictable Jimmy Smith (Verve)
The Cat (Verve)
Got My Mojo Workin' (Verve)

Jimmy Smith and Wes Montgomery
The Dynamic Duo (Verve)

Dr Lonnie Smith
Finger Lickin' Good (Columbia)
Think! (Blue Note)
Turning Point (Blue Note)
Drives (Blue Note)

Steve Swallow, featuring Carla Bley
Carla (XtraWATT)

The James Taylor Quartet
Mission Impossible (Jazid)
Money Spider (Jazid)
Get Organized (Polydor)
Do Your Own Thing (Polydor)

Uriah Heap, featuring Ken Hensley
Very 'Eavy, Very 'Umble (Vertigo)

Vanilla Fudge, featuring Mark Stein
Vanilla Fudge (Atco)

Various Artists
2B3: The Toronto Sessions (Maple)

Fats Waller
Fats Waller At The Organ Vol.3, 1926-29 (EPM Musique)

Bernie Worrell
Pieces Of Woo: The Other Side (CMP)
Funk Of Ages (Gramavision)

Tony Williams & Lifetime, featuring Larry Young
Emergency! (Verve)

Steve Winwood
Back In The High Life (Island)
About Time (Epic)

Yes, featuring Rick Wakeman
Fragile (Atlantic)
Close To The Edge (Atlantic)
Tales From Topographic Oceans (Atlantic)
Yessongs (Atlantic)

Larry Young
Unity (Blue Note)

Index

Picture credits

Rex

Fats Waller, Count Basie 5; Tori Amos, Sly & The Family Stone
21, 39; Rhoda Scott 43; Billy Preston 46; Graham Bond 49;
Brian Auger, Georgie Fame 50; Alan Price 53; Jon Lord 58;
Greg Allman 64; The Strawbs 69; The Zombies, Little Feat 72;
Tori Amos, Sam Yahel 93; Billy Preston 96; Brian Auger 97;
Jon Lord back cover.

Redferns

Jimmy Smith front cover; Steve Winwood 1; Wild Bill Davis 4;
Jimmy Smith 9; Keith Emerson 20; Jimmy Smith 23;
Jimmy McGriff 26; Brother Jack McDuff 30; Dr Lonnie Smith
35; Shirley Scott 36; Art Neville, Booker T. Jones 39, 42;
Bernie Worrell 43; Zoot Money 50; Manfred Mann 53;
Steve Winwood 57; Procol Harum, Pink Floyd 61; The
Grateful Dead 63; Keith Emerson 69; Santana 75; James Taylor
77; John Medeski 78; Barbara Dennerlein 82; Larry Goldings
87; Shirley Scott 97.